NOT
EVEN IN
BRAZIL

Jonathon Aspey

NOT EVEN IN BRAZIL

Liverpool in 1987/88

pitch

First published by Pitch Publishing, 2025

1

Pitch Publishing
9 Donnington Park,
85 Birdham Road,
Chichester, West Sussex,
PO20 7AJ
www.pitchpublishing.co.uk
info@pitchpublishing.co.uk

A CIP catalogue record is available for this book
from the British Library.

ISBN 978 1 80150 960 2

Typesetting and origination by Pitch Publishing

MIX
Paper | Supporting
responsible forestry
FSC
www.fsc.org
FSC® C013604

Printed and bound in the UK on FSC® certified paper in line
with our continuing commitment to ethical business practices,
sustainability and the environment.

Printed and bound by CPI Group (UK) Ltd, Croydon, CR0 4YY

Contents

Acknowledgements

WRITING A book had always been a dream of mine. When I wrote *Spice Up Your Life* several years ago, covering the story of Roy Evans's time as manager of Liverpool during the mid-1990s, I immediately wanted to write another – I just wasn't sure what about. I had previously written about Liverpool plenty of times, and the late 1980s period under Kenny Dalglish had been a particular area of focus for me. As a result, I couldn't stop myself, and decided to once again throw myself back into the glorious season that is Liverpool in 1987/88. Liverpool Football Club has always been special for me, and I'm truly privileged to have now worked with people involved with Liverpool much more closely than I am.

Firstly, I'd like to once again thank Pitch Publishing for being willing to publish my work. Thank you for being patient with me as I worked some things out, both with myself and the book. Your kindness and understanding did not go unnoticed as I worked through the challenge that this book has been. Secondly, I'd like to thank my wonderful wife. Thank you for all the times that we would put our daughter to bed and my first words to you would be, 'I'm going to write the book.' Thank you for so often sitting with me in our living room while I sat with the laptop on, blaring out games from the 1987/88 season. I know it hasn't been easy to lose that time, and please know that it is, and will always be appreciated by me. Thank you for the pep talks when I've needed them, as well as the reassuring words.

Thirdly, I want to say thank you to everyone at RedmenTV. You are a wonderful group of people who adore Liverpool Football Club in the best way. Thank you to Steve Plunkett for providing your memories of this season, as well as the other little nuggets of knowledge you've provided along the way. Dan Clubbe, thank you for the help you've tried to provide wherever possible, even if things haven't always worked out. Again, it is much appreciated. Thank you as well to Paul Moran and Angie Saunders for being willing to share their memories of what was an incredible season, and your writing provided what I wanted for the book, the fans' experience of Liverpool that season.

I also want to thank my grandad. As I've mentioned elsewhere in the book, my grandad passed away before this book could be completed, but I always told him he would feature in it. I wouldn't have known about this Liverpool side without him, and I'm truly gutted that he won't be able to read this book. I'll make sure I keep you a copy anyway. Thank you for passing your utter adoration for the wonderful game of football to me, and thank you for always asking about my progress and allowing me to tell you about what I had been watching and researching for the latest chapter I was writing. I miss you, and thank you so much.

Mum and Dad, as always, thank you for the support you've given me. Thank you for the encouragement that I could go and do whatever I wanted. Thank you for being so proud of me when I wrote *Spice Up Your Life*. I know neither of you particularly love football, so I look forward to seeing what you do with your latest copy of a book I've written. I hear they make excellent doorstops, although the dog would likely eat it.

Finally, to you the reader. Thank you for buying my book. This book has taken me some personal and professional challenges to write, but I'm very proud of what it has ended up being. I hope that whether you've seen Liverpool in 1987/88 before or not, this book transports you into that wonderful period in Liverpool's history, and that you ultimately enjoy reading it, as much as I enjoyed writing it. YNWA.

Thank you.

Preface

The Fan Experience – Anfield in 1987/88

THE 1987/88 season was my 19th of watching Liverpool Football Club, and I managed to go to 31 games, starting with a trip to Highfield Road in August to watch us beat Coventry City 4-1 with goals from Steve Nicol, John Aldridge (pen) and two from Peter Beardsley, and ending with what turned out to be a disastrous trip to Wembley in May for the FA Cup Final against Wimbledon. There was no Ian Rush in the attack for this season but his 'replacement', John Aldridge, who was signed earlier in 1987, came to the fore, especially with the prompting of new signings Beardsley and Barnes.

In my opinion, the style of football became much more adventurous, with some tremendous attacking play, but looking back at the games I went to, the defence kept 19 clean sheets. John Barnes was probably, at the time, the most exciting player I had seen playing for us, and the level of anticipation in the crowd when he got moving with the ball was something that I had not really experienced previously, even when Steve Heighway was in full flight.

If I was to pick my three favourite games from the season, they would be:

1. The 1-0 win over Everton at Goodison in the FA Cup, with Ray Houghton heading the winner.

2. The 3-3 draw at Anfield vs Manchester United, especially the two-goal burst from Peter Beardsley and Gary Gillespie that put us 2-1 in front after being 1-0 down.

3. The well-documented 5-0 win over Nottingham Forest at Anfield when we played some of the best football I have ever seen us produce in any of the over 1,200 live LFC games I have attended.

Unfortunately, the fact that we won the league that season was, for me, overshadowed by the defeat to Wimbledon in the FA Cup Final. It was always drummed into me by my dad not to anticipate victory in any game, but it was difficult not to approach this game, as a fan, wondering how many we would win by, although any previous game against them had usually been a scrappy, easily forgotten 90 minutes due to their 'unique' style of play. I have no doubts that the staff and players prepared for this game with totally the right attitude and mindset, and I believe it was a combination of bad luck and certainly at least one dreadful refereeing decision that cost us on the day, but the record books show that it was Wimbledon who were FA Cup winners in 1988, which rather reduces the effect of any bad luck stories.

Last point to mention was the fact that I think the 1-0 victory over Spurs when Peter Beardsley scored the winner is still, to this day, possibly the least-remembered title-winning game in the club's history.

Paul Moran

* * *

My best memory of that particular season is definitely the 5-0 win over Nottingham Forest, especially as it fell on my 18th birthday! One of my older brothers took me, and we sat in the Main Stand. For the whole match, the atmosphere was fantastic, and we just knew it was one of those special Anfield nights that would live on. We went to the pub afterwards and had a pretty good celebration!

The worst memory was the FA Cup Final. We all watched in our family home, and couldn't believe how it unfolded. Shock when they scored, shock when Aldo missed the penalty … it was awful. I'd never seen my dad in such a bad mood after that (until the Arsenal game the following year).

I found it hard to have a favourite player that season, the squad was fantastic, and all played their part. Kenny Dalglish has been my favourite player since he signed for us, and that is set in stone! However, Jan Mølby was my favourite then, he was fabulous, and such a good penalty taker. I still have the Jan Mølby pillowcase that my parents bought me then!

My mum allowed me to use the back of one of our doors to put up all my football pictures, postcards, etc. They were all up there, Steve McMahon, John Barnes, the lot. Sadly, we were away on holiday and my sister's then boyfriend (Evertonian) took it upon himself to deface every single one of them. There were speech bubbles, moustaches, glasses all over them. I was furious – and he never even replaced them!

Angie Saunders

* * *

Liverpool set about reclaiming their status at the top of English football. Our neighbours Everton were our chief rivals, having built up momentum over a largely successful period from '84 to '87, picking up silverware in the form of an FA Cup, Cup Winners' Cup and then First Division title the prior season. Exiting the club were Paul Walsh, John Wark and serial winner Mark Lawrenson, who sadly suffered an injury at Anfield versus Wimbledon that debilitated him and ended a stellar career. Added to the squad would be the mercurial Peter Beardsley and Ray Houghton from Newcastle and Oxford United, respectively. Allied to veterans Grobbelaar, Hansen, Whelan and player-boss Dalglish, who only contributed by way of two appearances, this was to all of us a squad capable of mounting a title challenge.

The attacking four of Ian Rush lookalike and score-a-like Aldridge, John Barnes, Peter Beardsley and Ray Houghton gave the perfect prelude as to what would follow by going to Highbury and coming away three points the richer. The winner came in the 88th minute from Steve Nicol, who would add goals to an already impressive list of attributes, which would include a hat-trick at St James' Park to spoil the 'Mirandinha' debut party.

With no defeats in the league at that stage, Liverpool went into battle with Everton on 1 November, goals from former blue McMahon and Beardsley giving Liverpool a statement win and the upper hand psychologically over our fiercest of rivals. It wasn't until 20 March that Liverpool lost their first league game. Everton were the victors as they tried to keep pace with Dalglish's all-conquering side and make a decent fist of their attempt to remain the top team in the division at the season's end. A further defeat at an emerging Nottingham Forest would be the second and final defeat of the season. The final table saw Liverpool secure a 17th league title by nine points.

Most pleasing for the Reds would be the Dalglish rebuild, the halcyon days of Souness and co. now cast into the annals of Liverpool football history, while this attack-minded Reds machine led by the exceptional and explosive John Barnes dared us to dream of the next ten years and what that trophy haul might look like.

Dalglish's rebuild and its subsequent success further cemented him as one of the all-time greats. He made astute signings and, when necessary, the same ruthless streak he demonstrated as a player would suffice.

League champions again and with panache and style, and not a sign of the old back-pass rule that served to stifle teams and their supporters alike. The task of reverting Everton to the title of second-best team on Merseyside was accomplished.

This was cavalier, and this was bloody marvellous. CHAMPIONS!

Steve Plunkett

Introduction

LIKE MANY, my love for football comes from my childhood. I remember as a young child getting up as early as I could every Sunday morning to watch *Match of the Day*.

I remember avidly adoring *Gazzetta Football Italia* on Channel 4 that has instilled in me to this day a deep-rooted love and passion not only for Italian football, but for Italy and Italian culture in general.

However, my number-one abiding memory of football from my childhood is a VHS tape. For those of you of a certain age reading this book, you know exactly what I'm talking about. For those of a younger disposition, it's what you call DVDs or Blu-Rays, but it was actually a tape that you put into a player, and it read what was on the tape inside the cassette and it played on your television. For the time, it was very, very advanced.

One day, and I don't even remember how old I was, or whether it was a birthday or Christmas present, my grandad gave me a *Goal of the Season* VHS that had been produced by the BBC. It contained all the goals of the season since the late 1960s, and it's undoubtedly where my interest in football history comes from. The VHS stopped in the 1993/94 season – I distinctly remember Ryan Giggs, Julian Joachim and Andy Cole goals featuring in that season – but as a young child there was one season that stood out to me above all others, and not just for the quality of goals that were scored, but because one team had been so good in that season that the BBC had dedicated all of the possible goals to vote for goal of the season to one club. That season was 1987/88, and the team was Liverpool.

As a child, I watched, mesmerised by the play of John Barnes, Peter Beardsley and John Aldridge, and the goals they scored. I still remember the incredible goal that Liverpool scored against Arsenal at Anfield, where Steve McMahon barely keeps the ball in play after running after it for what seems like an eternity, before slaloming past a sliding Arsenal boot and playing it inside for Beardsley, whose shot eventually creates the goal. This goal, and many others, are seminal moments in my football fandom, moments at which I became a child who not only liked football but was obsessed by it, and appreciated the aesthetic quality of football above all else. Since that point, I've always judged a football team by how much I enjoy watching them play, whether it was Jürgen Klopp's Liverpool or Pep Guardiola's Barcelona and it began with the Liverpool team of 1987/88.

So, this book is a love letter to that team, how it was developed over the previous years of management by Sir Kenny Dalglish, and how it swept away all others to win the First Division in a style that hadn't been seen for some time in English football. It's also a book that indirectly says thank you to my grandad, because without seeing that old VHS tape and seeing that great Liverpool team, my interest and appreciation for football might be quite different. During the latter part of the writing of this book, my grandad passed away at the age of 89. He read my first book, *Spice Up Your Life*, but he never got to read this one. If you're looking down Grandad, thank you, and I miss you.

This, *Not Even in Brazil: Liverpool in 1987/88*, is the story of that great season, the moments that led to it and the great games and goals that made it so memorable. Writing this book has been a wonderful experience, and I hope you enjoy reading about that team just as much as a younger version of me did watching those goals on that old VHS.

Chapter 1

Enter Dalglish

THE HEYSEL Stadium disaster is an event that will forever be remembered by Liverpool Football Club, and the impact of that event on Liverpool, Juventus, British and European football cannot be overstated. The relationship between English football and European football was damaged in a way that only Italia '90 would help fix. The tragic events of 29 May 1985, and the 39 souls who lost their lives, lived long in the memory of all who were present and witnessed the collapse of the separating wall, and the aftermath. In a truly rare example for football, the game became completely secondary, and shouldn't have been played. One of those present who was undoubtedly impacted by the disaster was the then Liverpool manager Joe Fagan. A long-term member of the fabled Boot Room, Fagan had become manager following the retirement of the legendary Bob Paisley in 1983, and had embarked on a fantastic run as Liverpool boss, with the 1983/84 season being one of the most legendary in the history of Liverpool Football Club. Months prior to the end of the 1984/85 season, Fagan had made the decision to retire, and had humanised himself to the players as soon as the game ended, telling them they could call him Joe, rather than 'Boss'. When Fagan stepped off the plane with fellow Boot Room coach Roy Evans, the emotional toll that Heysel had taken on him was clear for all to see.

From a footballing perspective, the question turned to how to replace another Boot Room member. In a few short years, the football club had said goodbye to Paisley and Fagan. In news that shocked some – although rumours had started to spread – the board announced just a day after Heysel on 30 May 1985, that 34-year-old Kenny Dalglish was set to become the first player-manager in the history of the Reds. Of course, Dalglish had known well in advance that he was making the step up, having almost been offered the job over the telephone by Peter Robinson. Despite Dalglish's undoubted status as a club legend, having scored 157 goals in the famous red kit, it has to be said that there were many who questioned the board's decision to replace Fagan with a man who was effectively a complete novice in management, even if by 1985 he had been a leader in the dressing room alongside figures such as Graeme Souness and Alan Hansen for years. However, Dalglish had Bob Paisley to turn to as an advisor, in a relationship that could only have helped him in the early days of his tenure at Anfield.

Dalglish's term in charge also started without European football. After finishing second to Howard Kendall's Everton in the 1984/85 season, Liverpool were supposed to be playing in the UEFA Cup in 1985/86. However, on 2 June 1985, UEFA banned all English clubs from competing in Europe and left English club sides in the European wilderness, an exile that would last until after the previously mentioned 1990 World Cup in Italy. Liverpool suffered greater punishment than the rest of English football, as they were given an additional three years on top of the European ban.

Dalglish also had to tackle the pressure that several of his former colleagues – who had become his underlings – were coming towards the end of their time at the club, and he needed to not only manage those egos on their way out of the club, but also find suitable and quality replacements that would see Liverpool into a new golden age with King Kenny at the helm. Not only that, but Dalglish needed to establish himself in a different role at Anfield and Melwood, with players that had become close colleagues and in many cases friends, such as Alan Hansen. Needless to say, the task that befell Kenny Dalglish in his first season as player-manager of Liverpool in 1985/86 was not insignificant. Incredibly, Dalglish went into the job with the practicality to say that if he performed below the expectations of a Liverpool manager, the board simply needed to cancel his contract as manager, and continue his contract as a player – on which he still had three years remaining. Dalglish would later state that he knew it would be difficult, and a huge change for the players.

One of the first big decisions made by Dalglish as manager was the selection of a new club captain. Full-back Phil Neal had been skipper at Anfield since the beginning of the 1984/85 season, and had won 50 caps for England at this point, having established himself as one of the best full-backs in Europe through the 1970s and 1980s. Despite this, Dalglish chose Alan Hansen as his captain – a decision that shocked the Scottish centre-back. With a reputation as one of the most elegant and skilful defenders in the history of the British game, Hansen became the dominant personality in an Anfield dressing room that was entering a new phase under Dalglish. Dalglish's reasoning for the change was: 'A captain has to be fortunate, has to be lucky, as well as good.' Dalglish's early decisions belied an innate managerial intuition that would serve him well throughout his tenure as Liverpool manager. However, Dalglish wouldn't make this decision permanent until partway through September, so as Liverpool's season began on 27 July 1985, Neal remained in place as skipper, with a testimonial scheduled for him in pre-season, although he continued to call Dalglish 'Kenny', rather than the agreed name of 'Boss'.

Neal's testimonial concluded an up and down pre-season schedule for the Reds, with dominant wins over Burnley, Brighton & Hove Albion and Charlton Athletic providing excitement for the red half of the city, but draws with Crewe Alexandra and Bristol City also received comments about the players looking 'lethargic'. Neal's testimonial was in a Merseyside derby with Everton, the Blues winning 3-2, despite Neal scoring from the penalty spot.

Without the Charity Shield to play for – league champions Everton defeated FA Cup winners Manchester United 2-0 at Wembley – Dalglish's first selection to face Arsenal in front of over 38,000 – the opening day of 1985/86 saw the lowest opening-day attendances since the war, clearly the impact of the negative press attention English football was receiving – at Anfield on the first matchday of the league campaign on 17 August 1985 was:

> Grobbelaar, Neal, Kennedy, Lawrenson, Whelan, Hansen, Dalglish, Nicol, Rush, Mølby, Beglin.

Steve Nicol and Jim Beglin were on the right and left flank, respectively, and both had a key role in Liverpool's opening-day victory, as Nicol scored Liverpool's second and assisted the first for Ronnie Whelan as Liverpool eased to a 2-0 victory, but they could have scored plenty more in the second half. Prior to the game, a service was held in remembrance of those lost in Brussels, and the Kop sang 'You'll Never Walk Alone', following the chorus of 'Abide with Me', although sound issues plagued the service itself.

The remainder of August saw Liverpool taste defeat only once, as they lost 1-0 to Jack Charlton's Newcastle United at St James' Park, but several dropped points saw the Reds sit eighth in the table, with draws away against West Ham United at the

Boleyn Ground, and Aston Villa at Villa Park. In several of those games, Liverpool were seemingly out of sorts, and Dalglish stated after the draw to West Ham, 'We have played three away games and lost five goals, and it has cost us seven points. Of those five goals four were from defensive errors, which is not good enough for any club, and certainly not Liverpool.'

Significant questions were being asked about Liverpool's playing staff early in Dalglish's tenure, and the biggest targets were Bruce Grobbelaar, the brilliant but eccentric man between the posts, and Phil Neal. Neal made way for Steve Nicol at right-back, his last appearance for Liverpool coming in November, before leaving the club in December to become player-manager of Bolton Wanderers. Dalglish and Liverpool knew Neal wanted to move into management and that he was disappointed not to have been offered the Liverpool job. As a result, the club didn't stand in his way. Further changes were also rumoured, with Liverpool linked to the all-action midfielder Steve McMahon. Dalglish was clearly looking to replace the box-to-box presence left by the departure of Graeme Souness from the club in 1984. McMahon officially signed with the Reds in September for a fee of £350,000 and went on to be a cornerstone of Dalglish's great side. Going the other way was Alan Kennedy, for £100,000 to Sunderland. A stalwart at left-back since making his debut in 1978, a poor start to the season saw Dalglish eventually replace him with Jim Beglin, as the legendary Bob Paisley's final Liverpool signing became the full-time left-back, shifting back from midfield.

Speaking of September, the month saw Liverpool unbeaten in the league, as the Reds dropped points only once, and quickly climbed up the table. Dalglish's side finished the month second in the First Division, and with the bragging rights of the city, having beaten league champions Everton at Goodison Park in one of the games of the season, with 51,000 at Goodison having the privilege of watching. Dalglish had given Jan Mølby the role of playing sweeper, and he thrived in the position, orchestrating Liverpool's play. Liverpool were lightning on the counter, and raced into a two-goal lead within 20 minutes through goals by Dalglish and Rush. McMahon made it 3-0 before half-time. Everton raced back late on in the second half, which brought the game to a terrific crescendo, but Liverpool held on, despite Dalglish uncharacteristically passing up some gilt-edged chances to extend Liverpool's lead, as he missed twice from point-blank range with Neville Southall already seemingly beaten. The only black cloud of the month was the runaway league leaders, Manchester United.

For the next two months, Liverpool continued their pace and maintained their position in second behind United, having won all but three times, with draws against Southampton and Chelsea and against United at Old Trafford. In Manchester, Dalglish's Reds had frankly battered Ron Atkinson's side, with the home team desperately lucky to come away without a beating. Liverpool did everything but win. To all, it simply seemed a matter of time before Liverpool took their rightful place at the top of the table, and English football in general, despite the ten-point gap that existed between first and second. November at least saw Liverpool get the victory over United they had so richly deserved at Old Trafford, when they welcomed the league leaders to Anfield in the Milk Cup. Mølby scored two goals in two minutes, the second being a penalty, but the first a glorious run from his own half, scything through a back-pedalling United defence, before he smashed the ball past United goalkeeper Gary Bailey from just outside the box.

However, it was not a merry Christmas for Liverpool, as they went on to have a horror show of a December, winning on 7 December against Aston Villa at Anfield, but going winless until 4 January. This included defeats against Arsenal at Highbury and Manchester City at Maine Road, as well as draws against Jack Charlton's Newcastle side – again – and Brian Clough's Nottingham Forest. Dalglish would later state that he felt the team were playing well enough, but they just weren't getting the results.

January saw a bounce back from the Reds, who went perfect through the rest of the month, which included wins in the Milk Cup and FA Cup to progress Liverpool through to the semi-final and fifth round, respectively. The six straight wins in January saw Liverpool score 19 goals and, as a result, Dalglish received the Manager of the Month award. Unfortunately, Liverpool's January purple patch came to a screeching halt, as they won only once in February, in an FA Cup fifth-round replay against Third Division side York City, winning 3-1 at Anfield after a 1-1 draw at Bootham Crescent. Most disappointing, however, was the 2-0 defeat to Everton at Anfield through goals by Kevin Ratcliffe – a shot from distance that was deflected and slowly squirmed under the body of Grobbelaar – and Gary Lineker – who had expertly broken the Liverpool offside trap to ease the ball past the Zimbabwean one on one. That defeat, for many, ended any hopes of challenging for a league title in Dalglish's first season. Even worse, the defeat took Everton top by three points, with Liverpool a further ten adrift.

Days later, Liverpool were knocked out of the Milk Cup by Queens Park Rangers in the semi-final after a 2-2 draw in the second leg, following a 1-0 defeat in the first. February of 1986 caused Alan Hansen to tell Dalglish that this was by a long distance the worst Liverpool team he'd ever played in. Liverpool also had injury concerns throughout February, with Dalglish himself unavailable at times, as well as forward Paul Walsh, who had ruptured his ankle ligaments in the 1-1 draw with Manchester United on 9 February, after enjoying a tempestuous start to life with Dalglish as player-manager, which had seen the pair verbally clash in the dressing room. Steve McMahon had also been unavailable for the nine matches before the Merseyside derby at Anfield. As bad as things looked after the derby for all those wearing red in the city, it was the last time Dalglish's Liverpool would lose all season.

You would have been forgiven for not immediately assuming that would happen, however, as Liverpool required an injury-time winner from Ian Rush to beat Spurs at the beginning of March, following another mistake by Bruce Grobbelaar that gave Tottenham the lead in the third minute. Nevertheless, it was the first Liverpool victory at White Hart Lane since 1975, and kept Dalglish's men in the title hunt, despite being eight points behind the blue half of Merseyside. Several reports stated that the player-manager had given the players an absolute rollocking at half-time. With Dalglish having not named himself in the first team, the creative responsibility laid at the talented feet of the Great Dane, Jan Mølby, and he duly repaid his manager, laying on assist after assist.

Dalglish returned to the line-up in Liverpool's next league match, however, as they gained quick revenge on Queens Park Rangers for knocking them out of the Milk Cup by battering them 4-1 at Anfield to climb to second in the table. Steve McMahon scored the first before Dalglish laid on a pair of assists, the first for his telepathic partner Ian Rush, the second for midfielder John Wark. McMahon scored his second in the 75th minute, with the assist being provided by Beglin from left-back. Despite McMahon's brace, the attention landed at the feet of the player-manager, who retained his ability to create from absolutely nothing, and set up the most difficult of goals in seemingly the easiest of ways.

Dalglish was a regular feature of the starting line-up as Liverpool's momentum built and built though the remainder of 1985/86.

A hectic fixture schedule throughout the rest of March 1986 saw Liverpool fail to win only twice, the first a 0-0 draw with Watford in the FA Cup sixth round at Anfield, with the visitors putting in a defensive performance that made life difficult for the Reds. Dalglish had implied on the day of the game that goals were highly likely, so a 0-0 draw was a surprise for the nearly 37,000 in attendance at Anfield. Despite being forced into a replay, a 2-1 win after extra time at Vicarage Road saw Liverpool through to the semis. Watford had taken the lead with a fantastic free kick from one John Barnes, the hyper-talented left-winger who terrified defences all across England, but Jan Mølby equalised from the penalty spot, and Rush scored in extra time to keep hopes alive of a Merseyside derby in the FA Cup Final.

Liverpool's second draw of the month was 0-0 against Sheffield Wednesday at Hillsborough in the First Division. Otherwise, all of Liverpool's other games that month were wins, against Southampton, Oxford United and Manchester City. Looking back, Alan Hansen stated that the team just began a run, and the momentum kept them going through the rest of the season. From being a team that looked well off the pace in February, the 2-0 win over City – with both goals scored by McMahon – saw Liverpool go top of the First Division by virtue of one goal difference, thanks to Everton's draw against Manchester United.

McMahon's second goal deserves specific mention as a great Liverpool goal, built from the back in the classic Liverpool style. Bruce Grobbelaar dropped the ball off to Hansen at the back, and the Scottish centre-back passed forwards to Ronnie Whelan in midfield. Whelan exchanged with Jim Beglin, who laid the ball inside to Hansen, who had moved up into midfield. Another progressive pass from Hansen was fired into the feet of Dalglish, who executed a deft flick to lay the ball to Jan Mølby, who moved it out to the right flank to Craig Johnston with one touch. From there, Johnston fired in a hard, low cross that met McMahon at the back post, and the midfielder's sliding finish saw the ball fizz past Barry Siddall in the City net. Liverpool are a team with a history of scoring great goals, but this one ranks pretty highly, and was a taster of the aesthetic beauty that Dalglish's team would go on to achieve in later years.

At the other end of the pitch, since the two-legged defeat to QPR in the Milk Cup, Liverpool had only conceded three goals. What's more, the club had seen the emergence of Gary Gillespie, who had partnered Hansen excellently, as he began to stake his claim for the ever-dependable Mark Lawrenson's place in defence.

April 1986 began with Liverpool again needing to go to extra time to progress in the FA Cup, and it was again the ever-dependable Ian Rush that was the Reds' saviour at White Hart Lane, as he scored twice after 90 minutes against Southampton to send Liverpool through to the final at Wembley. They were set to face none other than Everton in the last game of the season on 10 May. From nowhere, Liverpool found themselves in with a chance of winning the club's first-ever league and cup double, and the first in English football since Arsenal achieved the feat in 1970/71.

Dalglish's side followed up the FA Cup semi-final with a 5-0 victory over Coventry City as they returned to league action at Anfield. Ronnie Whelan bagged himself a hat-trick, as the Reds now looked peerless, unstoppable, brilliant – whichever adjective you care to assign them. Despite Liverpool's incredible form, Everton continued to win, firstly against Arsenal and then Watford, to keep their noses just ahead, but Dalglish's team also continued to win, beating Luton Town 1-0 at Kenilworth Road on the astroturf surface. Three days later, a poor Liverpool performance at The Hawthorns against West Bromwich Albion required the individual brilliance of both Dalglish and Rush to secure a 2-1 victory that kept them top of the First Division. When Everton failed to beat Brian Clough's Nottingham Forest days later, the door swung wide open for Liverpool to achieve breathing space at the top.

Liverpool marched their way through the door with a 5-0 victory at Anfield over Birmingham City that saw Gary Gillespie score an unlikely hat-trick. This performance demonstrated quite clearly how far Dalglish's side – and therefore Dalglish himself – had come in just nine months, looking more than worthy champions as they marched towards a richly deserved league title. When Everton succumbed to defeat against Oxford United, and Liverpool won in their next game against Leicester City – Oxford's win caused quite the celebration in the Kop – with goals by Rush and Whelan, it meant a draw against Chelsea in their final game would effectively bring the First Division trophy back across Stanley Park, with Howard Kendall's men unlikely to overturn the huge goal difference Liverpool had amassed. Having said that, Alan Hansen would later admit that Liverpool at the time had a poor away record at Chelsea's Stamford Bridge. Despite the record, confidence was high in the red side of Liverpool heading into the final day. Meanwhile, Howard Kendall said, 'Suddenly, I'm a Chelsea supporter,' as he and his reigning league champions found fate out of their own hands on the final day.

Anfield legend and stalwart Jan Mølby found himself unable to play in the decider, failing a late fitness test, but his place in the back three was taken by Mark Lawrenson. Chelsea started well, with Liverpool barely getting the ball for the first five minutes of the game, but eventually the Reds settled and began to show the football they had played in the latter half of the 1985/86 season. Midway through the first half, Liverpool pushed forwards, having a Jim Beglin shot cleared off the line and out for a throw-in. Craig Johnston took the throw towards Gary Gillespie, who flicked it on, but the ball was cleared away, only as far as Ronnie Whelan. Whelan then tried a shot that ricocheted off a Chelsea leg into the path of Beglin, whose weighted pass found Kenny Dalglish just inside the box. In typical Dalglish fashion, King Kenny chested the ball into his path, and his guided right-foot volley found the bottom corner of the Chelsea net as Tony Godden came out to save. As Dalglish wheeled away to celebrate, he was on the verge of becoming the first-ever player-manager to win the First Division. As the commentary team said, the manager was leading by example.

Chelsea pushed forwards in search of an equaliser in the second half, but when the final whistle went after the 90 minutes, Kenny Dalglish's Liverpool had once again reclaimed their position at the very top of English football, when so many had written them off earlier in the season, and had written off Dalglish as manager, in particular. In the hours after lifting the trophy as both player and manager, Dalglish stated that he'd had plenty of help along the way – and to be fair, he had, from Bob Paisley, Ronnie Moran, Roy Evans and Tom Saunders – but that modesty was typical of Dalglish, who had the Manager of the Year award for 1985/86 bestowed upon him. Dalglish had done what many others would have failed to do, steady the ship after the retirement of Joe Fagan and the spectre of Heysel, and had begun to rebuild the Liverpool side. To do so *and* win a league title was quite an achievement that should not be understated in the great seasons in Liverpool's history – even if it's not the season this book will focus on most. Of course, there was still the double to go for, in a Merseyside derby at Wembley.

Merseyside emptied for the 1985/86 FA Cup Final, as tens of thousands of Liverpudlians made their way south to London for the game. It was the first Merseyside derby in the history of the FA Cup Final. The city became a sea of red and blue, as each household – and indeed bedroom – demonstrated the side of Stanley Park they held allegiance to. Given everything that the city of Liverpool withstood through the 1980s – poverty, drugs, tensions in the Labour Party over the Liverpool council, Margaret Thatcher's Conservative government – the game meant more than just a normal FA Cup Final, or even a normal Merseyside derby. Chants of 'Scousers here, Scousers there, Scousers every-fucking-where' and 'Merseyside, Merseyside' were heard throughout the day, as Liverpool and Everton fans took the opportunity to unite in demonstration of unity and collective support. Only in Liverpool.

Dalglish's side for the FA Cup Final was:

Grobbelaar, Nicol, Lawrenson, Hansen, Beglin, Johnston, Mølby, MacDonald, Whelan, Dalglish, Rush.

Officially there were 98,000 at Wembley. Liverpool started well but it was Everton who came into the game more through the first half and had claims for a penalty turned down by the official Alan Robinson. However, minutes later, Peter Reid put Player of the Year Gary Lineker through on goal. He beat Alan Hansen in a foot race, and although Grobbelaar saved Lineker's initial effort, the England striker scored the rebound and gave the Toffees the lead in the final. Everton went in at half-time very much in the ascendancy, not only on the scoresheet but on the field.

The blue side of the city began the second half just as well, and Liverpool looked rattled and struggled to maintain possession, so much a cornerstone of their play. Liverpool's defence looked shaky, with Grobbelaar frightening Reds all across the country as he fumbled a Kevin Sheedy cross, before he eventually regained the ball and screamed in the face of Jim Beglin. Minutes later, a poor Grobbelaar clearance saw him on the receiving end of some choice words from Dalglish, with he and Rush merely spectators at that point in the game.

Seconds later, an intercepted Everton clearance saw Whelan play the ball inside to Mølby, who slipped it through the Everton offside trap, and the on-running Ian Rush collected the ball, went round Bobby Mimms in the Everton net, and scored the equaliser to make it 1-1, after Liverpool had just endured their worst spell of the game.

Suddenly, Liverpool looked like Liverpool again. Their first touches weren't so poor, and confidence flooded back into the side. What had been a game with Everton absolutely dominating and looking to kill it off, became very much 'game on'. After a brief scare as Grobbelaar wonderfully saved a Graeme Sharp effort by tipping it over the bar, Liverpool came forwards down the left through Rush. He passed inside to Mølby, just on the edge of the box. Showing speed of thought that rivalled anyone in English football in that era, Mølby moved the ball to his left and fired towards the back post, where suddenly Craig Johnston found himself free to tap the ball into an empty half of the net. 2-1 Liverpool. Twenty minutes later, as Everton pushed forwards for an equaliser, Kevin MacDonald won the ball in midfield and laid the ball off to Ronnie Whelan, who lofted a pass out to the right flank for Johnston, who flicked it forwards to Rush. As he picked the ball up on the move, Rush moved into midfield still in the Liverpool half and laid it off to Mølby, who was sitting within the centre-circle. As Everton defenders quickly looked to close down the Great Dane, Ronnie Whelan overlapped him to the left, and collected the ball as Liverpool now marched into Everton's half. Just outside Everton's box, Whelan held his run and lofted the ball to Rush, who had made a run into the far side of the Everton area. In classic Rush fashion, he needed two touches: one to control, and the second to fire in Liverpool's third goal, a goal that secured the first double in English football since 1970/71.

As the red contingent within Wembley began to celebrate, the minutes ticked away until Liverpool were confirmed as double winners. As Alan Hansen walked up the famous Wembley steps to collect the FA Cup, Dalglish's Liverpool had put the icing on the cake of a truly fantastic season, one that promised much for the Scot's tenure in the Anfield dugout.

As good as things seemed on the red side of Liverpool – and they were – Dalglish still had to add some youth to the team, and retain Ian Rush, who had begun to attract more and more interest from Italy, with Inter Milan rumoured to be interested.

As 1985/86 bled into 1986/87, Dalglish knew that Everton would be back stronger and looking to reclaim the league title, and admitted that repeating the incredible double of 1985/86 would be quite a task. It was made a little easier by Everton's loss of star striker – and 1986 World Cup Golden Boot winner – Gary Lineker, who jetted off to Terry Venables's Barcelona for £2.75m, but the main story of the summer on the red side of the city would be the sale of Liverpool's own star striker, Ian Rush, as he signed a £3.2m deal to leave for Serie A, a British record fee. It was the Italian champions Juventus signing Rush rather than Inter Milan, but the Welshman's transfer left a gaping hole in the Liverpool starting line-up that Dalglish and the board had to fill. Rush remained with the club for the 1986/87 season on loan, while Juventus sorted out their quota of foreign players, but come 1987/88, Liverpool needed to have a plan to replace his goals and spend most, if not all of the £3.2m fee.

Dalglish began to invest through the summer as he spent £200,000 to sign right-back Barry Venison from Sunderland. Still in his early 20s, Venison had first attracted interest in 1983/84, but a year after the North East club's relegation to the Second Division, Venison wrote to Liverpool, touting his services. His signing provided competition for places and gave him the chance to become the first-choice right-back. A further £70,000 went to Irish club Dundalk to sign 17-year-old Steve Staunton, who went on to be a key part of Dalglish's side in his latter years at Anfield. However, for those who likely expected the money to be spent immediately, Venison and Staunton weren't additions that would have caused significant improvement to the side. Then again, this was a team that had just won the double, and Rush wasn't set to leave for another year, which made the search for a replacement less urgent, but no less important.

The club made only one sale other than Rush, and it was the departure of Sammy Lee, who joined Queens Park Rangers for £200,000. Lee had been a first-team regular in the early 80s, but had gradually found himself beneath Kevin MacDonald and Craig Johnston in the midfield pecking order. He later returned to Anfield in a coaching capacity, and was part of Graeme Souness's backroom staff in the 1990s, and would remain at the club under the tenures of Roy Evans and Gérard Houllier.

As it ended in 1985/86, Liverpool's season began against Everton at Wembley, for the Charity Shield. Dalglish started the game on the bench as he selected Rush to start as a lone centre-forward, with a collection of Kevin MacDonald, Craig Johnston, Steve McMahon, Ronnie Whelan and Jan Mølby behind him. Also there to see Rush was Juventus president Giampiero Boniperti, and he would likely have come away impressed at his latest signing for the Bianconeri. Dalglish also selected Venison to start at right-back. Dalglish's self-benching has to be seen as early signs of his desire to phase himself out of the side as part of the rebuilding, but after a first half that yielded little success for the Reds, the 35-year-old player-manager brought himself on in the 65th minute, later joking that half an hour was the most he could manage. Nevertheless, Dalglish stated that he wouldn't pick anyone based on sentiment, least of all himself.

His introduction, however, sparked some life into the Liverpool side, which had also lost Bruce Grobbelaar to injury in the second half, but in truth the Zimbabwean keeper had been hobbling for a decent portion of the game. Dalglish's introduction saw almost immediate improvement from Liverpool as Rush blazed over the bar from a lethal counter-attack, but it was Everton that took the lead after Hansen was beaten in the air by Graeme Sharp, and Adrian Heath almost instinctively ran on to the ball and into the box to fire past Mike Hooper into the far corner.

Everton had chances to secure the win, but three minutes from time a Jim Beglin free kick on the halfway line found Dalglish on the edge of the box.

Dalglish nodded the ball back to Mølby, who himself nodded it forwards into the mass of bodies. Then, seemingly out of nowhere, Craig Johnston flicked the ball with his heel on the half-volley into the path of Rush, who volleyed the ball first time out to the right-hand side of the box into the path of Kenny Dalglish. Dalglish then cut the ball back into the six-yard box, meeting the onrushing – no pun intended, but happily discovered – Ian Rush, who side-footed the ball into the net to make it 1-1. It was the kind of magic that Liverpool always seemed to be able to find, just when they needed it. With only minutes left when Rush equalised, the match ended 1-1, with the Charity Shield shared for 1986/87.

As the teams posed for pictures together in yet another example of Merseyside solidarity, the match itself did highlight some warning signs for Dalglish's team, and the club in general. Ultimately, it had been individual quality that had brought Liverpool level, and Rush was leaving at the end of the season, while, at 35, Dalglish surely had to be thinking of how he would replace his own play in the team, a job that was no mean feat. Another big concern was that this was hardly a full-strength Everton side, as injuries had affected Howard Kendall's selection, and it included new signings who still needed to settle in.

Liverpool began their 1986/87 season away from Anfield in the North East, as they faced Newcastle United at St James' Park. Kenny Dalglish again started himself on the bench, and Liverpool were missing Bruce Grobbelaar too, who was unavailable until the end of September. Still, Liverpool had Ian Rush, and he scored twice to give the Reds a fantastic start to their league campaign, despite being partnered with Ronnie Whelan in what many called a 'make-do and mend' Liverpool. A better team than Newcastle may have given the Reds more of a fight, with only Peter Beardsley, who had shone at that summer's World Cup, looking a threat to Liverpool's defence.

Liverpool went unbeaten throughout the rest of the month of August, as Dalglish returned to the starting line-up to partner Rush up front in the 4-4-2. However, unbeaten makes things sound a little better than they were. Manchester City had been more than deserving of their 0-0 draw with Liverpool at Anfield, and Arsenal showed plenty of promise despite being beaten 2-1, and Liverpool had the goals and performances of Rush and Mølby to thank. With Rush on his way to Turin, rumours also began to spread that Juventus were interested in signing Mølby to join him. Dalglish had said to the press earlier in the month that he wished Juventus hadn't come in for Rush, and he certainly wouldn't have been keen on them taking the Great Dane as well. Rush had actually received the first red card of his career after the City game, as he apparently swore at an official on his way off the pitch, but this was later rescinded, so the Welshman's record remained unblemished.

However, September saw Liverpool's record – and unbeaten run that stretched back to February – blemished by a 2-1 defeat to Leicester City at Filbert Street, as Dalglish's side – with the Scotsman on the bench – struggled to cope with Leicester's sweeper system. Incredibly, Liverpool's loss didn't see Everton go top of the First Division, but surprise package Wimbledon.

Liverpool bounced back with a 5-2 victory over West Ham United at Upton Park, but it required an Alan Hansen injury to bring Dalglish on to the pitch, which turned the game around for the Reds. Hansen was out of action for most of the month. Liverpool ended September fifth in the table following a second league defeat, this time at The Dell against Southampton, as Rush and Dalglish scored for Liverpool, but a Mike Hooper error gifted Southampton the three points. Dalglish's side followed that up with a 3-3 draw against Aston Villa, as the returning Grobbelaar took his turn to make a crucial mistake that dropped points. At least Liverpool had more luck in the League Cup, where they beat Fulham 10-0 – yes, ten – at Anfield in the first leg that all but guaranteed progress to the third round. Liverpool also won the ScreenSport Super Cup in September. Hang on, what?

Following the banning of English clubs from European competition following the tragedy at Heysel Disaster, the Football League had come up with the ingenious idea to have all the clubs who had qualified for European football in the 1984/85 season play in a Super Cup that replaced the European games – and in theory, money – that they were missing out on due to the UEFA ban. This had started in the 1985/86 season, and had been little more than an inconvenience to teams that they had to fit around their league and FA Cup responsibilities. Howard Kendall is famous for saying to his players before one Super Cup game, 'What a waste of time this is – out you go.' Nevertheless, Liverpool reached the final of said tournament and faced an injury-ravaged Everton, who had conveniently been placed in the other half of the draw. Attendances had been low, and interest was even lower across the country, with the FA Cup at its peak in terms of reputation, and the League Cup still a respected competition. Liverpool won 7-2 on aggregate to win the first, and only, ScreenSport Super Cup in what was a truly forgettable moment in the history of English football.

As they returned to league action in October, Dalglish's Liverpool continued to stutter and stumble as they lost twice in the First Division and continued to fall behind the league leaders. The first was to Tottenham Hotspur at Anfield, a Clive Allen goal winning what was reported as a fantastic game of football in front of a brilliant Anfield crowd, something that was much needed after the 1986 Conservative Party Conference that had associated football hooliganism – and therefore football fans – with picketing, as Margaret Thatcher's war with the unions continued in the wake of the miners' strike of 1984–85. Despite wins in their other First Division games that month, a 4-1 defeat away at Kenilworth Road against Luton Town left the Reds fifth in the table.

A bright spot was the continued progress in the League Cup, as Liverpool beat Leicester City 4-1 at Anfield through a Steve McMahon hat-trick, and Dalglish scored the other. At the very least, November saw Liverpool unbeaten, as Dalglish's men began to pick up momentum as they headed into the difficult Christmas months. Nevertheless, when a Dalglish-less Liverpool won 2-0 against Coventry City on 29 November with goals by Jan Mølby and John Wark, they only sat third in the table. Surprisingly, they were a point ahead of Everton, with Brian Clough's Nottingham Forest in second, and George Graham's Arsenal leading the pack.

By the end of Christmas 1986, Liverpool still sat third, but had dropped yet more points, having lost against Watford and, painfully, Manchester United at Anfield. The most noticeable change at Anfield over the winter months was the decline in appearances of one Kenny Dalglish. He had started plenty of matches as the season began but, as 1986/87 progressed, Dalglish began to name himself on the bench more often, and at times didn't even do that. It was becoming increasingly clear that Dalglish felt the need to phase himself out of the side, and he looked to bring replacements into the team. One example was Paul Walsh, who had returned from his ankle injury in October. Dalglish was also experimenting more with Liverpool's tactics, as he at times played a back three and used three midfielders. However, he often returned to the classic 4-4-2 formation that was so well understood by the players.

In what has become a marker of so many of the great teams over the decades in English football, Liverpool began to really kick into gear after Christmas, and went unbeaten in the league through January and February 1987, climbing to second in the table. The foundation of the recovery was the defence, which recorded nine clean sheets in a two-month stretch in all competitions. The only disappointing result was once again slipping up against Luton Town on their artificial pitch at Kenilworth Road, in a 3-0 defeat in the FA Cup third-round replay, meaning Dalglish's men had only the league and the League Cup to fight for. January had also seen Liverpool lose left-back Jim Beglin, as he broke his leg after a horrific tackle from Everton's Gary Stevens. The leg break was awful for everyone at the club. Bob Paisley said of the injury, 'I've seen one or two broken legs in going on 50 years in the game, but not one made me really wince. Jim's did.' Sadly, it was the last appearance Beglin would make in a Liverpool shirt, and he left on a free transfer after the 1988/89 season.

The Reds opened March with a 2-0 win over their bogeymen Luton Town at a snow-filled Anfield, which saw them finally return to the top of the table, by two points from Everton – as Arsenal dropped off in third. However, Everton had a key game in hand on Dalglish's Reds. On the bench in that game was new recruit John Aldridge, a forward signed from Oxford United for £750,000 who had scored 15 goals in 25 games so far in the 1986/87 season. Clearly, Aldridge had been signed by Dalglish to replace the departing Kop legend Ian Rush, but for now had to make do with the bench, despite the fact that he started and scored in Liverpool's 1-0 win over Southampton at Anfield at the end of February. Aldridge didn't make much of a mark for the remainder of the season, but Dalglish told the forward to wait and be patient, and he would sign players who would be more suited to his style of play as a great back-to-goal link-up man and leader of the line. Also signed that winter was the tenacious and versatile midfielder Nigel Spackman, who joined from Chelsea for £400,000 and went on to be a key part of the midfield through the remainder of 1986/87 and 1987/88.

An Ian Rush-inspired 1-0 win over former league leaders Arsenal on 10 March saw Liverpool temporarily go six points clear of the blue side of Merseyside. Mark Lawrenson came back into the centre of defence for the game, with first-choice Gary Gillespie unavailable due to being injured. Nevertheless, having a player of the quality of Mark

Lawrenson to come into the team was a luxury that very few clubs in English football could afford. Two further wins followed, against Oxford United and Queens Park Rangers, as it looked as if Dalglish's Liverpool were starting to stretch their legs towards another league triumph, nine points clear of Everton in second.

Then it all fell apart. All of a sudden, the team that had looked in imperious form since the turn of the year, with Rush having scored several key goals that kept them top of the table, just collapsed. Defeats against Tottenham and Wimbledon started to cause concern, especially when they were followed up by defeat at Wembley in the League Cup Final against Arsenal. To add insult to developed injury, Liverpool then lost a fourth game, and a third league game on the bounce, with defeat against Norwich City. The 2-1 reverse at Carrow Road saw Liverpool slip to second, and their hated rivals Everton overtook them.

The turnaround had been so fast, and Liverpool's form so bad, that after a 1-0 defeat against Manchester United at Old Trafford on 20 April, defeat in their next game, the Merseyside derby against Everton, would have handed the First Division trophy to Howard Kendall's men. Fortunately, Dalglish's side put in a much improved performance and beat the Blues 3-1 at Anfield. Naturally, the scorer of two of Liverpool's three goals was Ian Rush, who equalled Dixie Dean's goalscoring record in Merseyside derbies. However, the win was effectively a stay of execution, and when Liverpool once again fell to defeat in their following game against Coventry at Highfield Road, the league title went to the blue half of Liverpool for the second time in three years.

The last two games of the season saw Rush score against Watford in his final home appearance before his departure to Juventus, and a high-scoring 3-3 draw against Chelsea at Stamford Bridge. Definitely of note ahead of the 1987/88 season, however, was the sharpness of John Aldridge, who was selected in the starting line-up against Chelsea and repaid Dalglish with a goal and an assist. Also of note was that not only was the Watford game Rush's last appearance before his journey to Italy, but it was also the final time Kenny Dalglish was named as a starter for Liverpool Football Club. Indeed, Dalglish only made two appearances for the club in the coming season. Effectively, King Kenny's playing career was all but over. Through the first half of the 80s, Anfield had been able to rely on the partnership of Dalglish and Rush. Now, suddenly, that was gone. Needless to say, this really was a major turning point in the history of the club.

It was clear that the change that Dalglish had been slowly building towards needed to happen more quickly. Prior to the run of form that saw Liverpool win the league and cup double in 1985/86, Alan Hansen had actually said it was 'the worst Liverpool side I'd ever played in'. Liverpool had lost the league title to their hated neighbours twice in three years, and in truth it had been a simply incredible run of form in 1985/86 that had seen them leapfrog Everton to win the title. Liverpool couldn't be expected to make that comeback every single season. The team's reliance on Rush and Dalglish was no longer possible as the Welshman jetted off to Serie A and the Scot entered an almost self-inflicted retirement as a player.

It's true that Dalglish had already committed to rebuilding the team – and had recognised very early in his tenure that change was needed – bringing in players such as Gary Gillespie, Steve McMahon, Barry Venison, Nigel Spackman and, most importantly, John Aldridge. However, the decline in Liverpool's play towards the end of the season told the real story, that while Dalglish had done good work through his first two years in charge of rebuilding the Reds – and had arguably more than overachieved in 1985/86 – more changes were required at Anfield in order to avoid the club falling behind Everton, and the balance of power shifting more permanently on Merseyside. The task that faced Kenny Dalglish heading into the next league campaign was no small feat, and the Kop faithful expected Liverpool to be back in 1987/88. They would see a season for the ages.

Chapter 2

The Summer and Pre-Season

FOLLOWING THE disappointment that was
the end of the 1986/87 season, Kenny Dalglish and
Liverpool Football Club entered the summer of 1987
knowing full well that improvements were needed at
Anfield. Gone was the ultimate talisman Ian Rush,
who had joined Italian champions Juventus for £3.2m,
with his one-year loan to remain in Merseyside now
over. What's more, Dalglish had severely reduced
his own playing time through 1986/87, as the club
legend evidently became aware of his own decline as a
player, but also the need for them to move into a new
phase, and hopefully a new era of dominance over
English football. Part of the £3.2m from Rush's sale
had already been invested back into the playing staff,
but with city neighbours Everton having won two
league titles in three years, Arsenal improving under
George Graham, and Manchester United surely to

come good at some point under relative newcomer Sir Alex Ferguson – despite some significant early troubles – Liverpool were not quite as secure on their perch as they had been only three or so years earlier.

First through the door at Melwood was perhaps the most important signing Dalglish would make in his entire spell as manager of Liverpool from 1985–1991. For what would now be considered – even with inflation considered – a stupendous bargain at £900,000, Liverpool signed the Watford left-winger John Barnes. Barnes, who was born in Jamaica, had emigrated to Britain when his father was appointed Jamaica's military attaché in London. Upon arriving in Britain at the age of 13, John soon found himself a football club, joining Stowe Boys Club. Having initially played in midfield or up front in Jamaica, Barnes incredibly ended up playing as a centre-half for Stowe. Still at youth level, Barnes was spotted by Graham Taylor, who reported having seen him score with a left-footed shot. He then left, saying, 'That's all I need to see.' With Taylor's pioneering, if direct, football that Barnes seemed incredibly suited to down the left, he would go on to become one of the most entertaining players in Britain, being named in Sir Bobby Robson's England squad for the 1986 World Cup, and tearing the Argentina defence to shreds after coming on in the infamous Hand of God quarter-final. Dalglish had clearly been interested in Barnes for some time, specifically telling Alan Hansen back in December 1986 after a 2-0 defeat at Vicarage Road – where Barnes had beaten Hansen to score Watford's second – that he was going to sign Barnes.

Despite his quite obvious quality, Barnes was labelled by the media as a step away from the established Liverpool format, perhaps for the fact that, unlike many of Liverpool's wide players over the years, he was a legitimate winger who wanted to pick the ball up and drive at the opposition, using his pace, physicality and immense creativity to often leave defenders looking ridiculous as he stormed by them. Bob Paisley would question whether people believed that Barnes's skill and flamboyance would mix with the understated machine that Liverpool had become through the 70s and 80s. The Liverpool legend would state very clearly that Liverpool's machine relied on talent and ability above all others, and that he believed their new signing had that in abundance. He accurately identified that every team that faced Liverpool throughout the 1987/88 season would have one priority, to 'Keep John Barnes quiet.' Many would fail at this singular task.

Interestingly, Barnes had believed that Dalglish intended to play him up front alongside John Aldridge when he joined, but when he asked the still technically player-manager where he would be playing, Dalglish immediately responded, 'Left wing.' Despite that, Dalglish would give Barnes immense creative freedom throughout the season, with the winger free to come narrow and combine with the midfielders and forwards.

The reason for Barnes playing on the left was that, after two seasons of seemingly wanting to remove himself from the side, Dalglish had finally replaced himself as the creator in Liverpool's strike partnership. Eight days after the signing of Barnes, Liverpool signed Peter Beardsley from Newcastle United for a British record fee of £1.9m. Beardsley had gone through quite the journey to arrive at Anfield, starting his career in the Third Division with Carlisle United, before playing in the North American Soccer League with the Vancouver Whitecaps from 1981–83, with a short stint at Manchester United sandwiched in that period of time. Beardsley would only make one appearance for the Red Devils, though, and ended up in the North East in 1983 with Newcastle United. There he would immediately become a favourite of the Geordie faithful and, like Barnes, was named in Sir Bobby Robson's 1986 World Cup squad, where he forced his way into the side as a perfect partner for Golden Boot winner Gary Lineker.

During this period, Beardsley had helped Newcastle gain promotion to the First Division, but the North East club continued to struggle – as it had throughout the 1980s – finishing only three points above the relegation zone in the 1986/87 season. With only a year remaining on his contract with Newcastle, the writing was on the wall, and Beardsley was put up for sale. In something resembling fate, the then Newcastle manager Willie McFaul rejected a £2m offer from Manchester United, and instead sold Beardsley to Liverpool.

There was no doubt that Dalglish was well aware of the calibre of player he had signed, and the impact he would go on to have for Liverpool. Beardsley would later state that Dalglish himself had instructed him to ask for more money when negotiating with the club, as he deserved to be paid as a top player at the top club in England. Weeks after agreeing a deal with Newcastle, the North East club finally gave Beardsley permission to speak to Dalglish. After a comical tour of the North West to avoid the media, Beardsley agreed terms with Liverpool within an hour, and Dalglish had the attacking trident that would do so much damage in 1987/88: John Barnes, Peter Beardsley and John Aldridge. Amazingly, in December 1986, the board had approached Dalglish and said money was available for players. With the manager showing incredible foresight, Barnes, Beardsley and Aldridge were three of the five players that he requested, with a fourth that would join early in the season. Dalglish had made the decision to wait until his first-choice options were available, and it more than paid off for him.

Liverpool's pre-season began in West Germany on 23 July, as they travelled to Munich to be part of the testimonial that Bayern Munich were holding for Dieter Hoeneß. Liverpool were uncharacteristically quiet in the game that ended 3-2 to the German hosts, but Dalglish's selection was a mix of old and new faces, according to Phil McNulty writing in the *Liverpool Echo*. Still, the game saw Barnes score a late goal to make the game appear closer than it was, and Beardsley was able to get a run out in the red shirt for the first time, after training with the club for a week following his transfer.

The pre-season really kicked off with a tour of Scandinavia that saw Dalglish's men go unbeaten after facing Aalborg Chang, Brønshøj BK, Vejle,

Karlstad BK and Vålerenga in games across Denmark, Sweden and Norway. The tour saw Dalglish at times experiment with his line-up, including playing Beardsley in central midfield in their first game, but as the tour went on Beardsley settled into his customary spot alongside Aldridge up front, with Barnes on the left wing to terrorise and torment opposition right-backs. This meant that Liverpool lined up in a very settled, but fluid, 4-4-2 formation.

Returning to the British Isles, Liverpool's next game was another testimonial, this time for Tommy Burns of Celtic, as 42,000 turned up at Parkhead to watch Liverpool beat Celtic 1-0 in a match that earned Burns well over £100,000. Dalglish would even substitute himself on in the second half, receiving thunderous applause from the Celtic faithful. Perhaps interestingly, given much of the controversy and discussion around fans – particularly Liverpool fans – following Heysel, reports of expected crowd trouble turned out to be completely false in a well-mannered game that saw Celtic rarely threaten the goal of Bruce Grobbelaar. Next followed a 5-0 win against the Irish Olympic squad at Lansdowne Road, which saw a fantastic performance from Peter Beardsley. Then came a 1-0 win over Atlético Madrid that demonstrated Liverpool's ability in comparison to their European competition, with centre-back pairing Alan Hansen and Gary Gillespie more than handling Atlético's new €5.50m signing Paulo Futre. Barnes was inspired on the left wing as well, but Dalglish refused to be drawn into any further discussion of his team's performance. However, it was a clear indication of what his side were going to be capable of in the 1987/88 First Division.

When that game was played on 23 August, Liverpool's First Division campaign was already eight days old, but they would need to wait until 12 September to return to Anfield. In July, a sewer underneath the famous Kop that stretched back to the 1860s had collapsed, opening up a huge hole measuring 20ft by 15ft in the middle of the stand, and it would require £100,000 of investment to repair. While Anfield's preparations for the new league season may have hit somewhat of a snag, the team's certainly hadn't. The trio of Barnes, Beardsley and Aldridge looked ready to unleash on English football, and Liverpool seemed completely refreshed in comparison to their sluggish form through major parts of the 1986/87 season. Anfield, and English football, were about to be witness to a season that's not only arguably the best-ever league season on Merseyside, but in the entirety of English football.

Chapter 3

The Start: August and September

WITH THE sewer issues meaning that Liverpool wouldn't make an appearance at Anfield until September, the Reds began their 1987/88 First Division campaign with three consecutive away fixtures, and opening the league season with the most difficult of the three, as they visited north London to face Arsenal.

George Graham's side were continuing to make progress as they built what would eventually become a title-winning team in 1988/89, coming fourth in 1986/87 as well as beating Dalglish's Reds in the League Cup Final at Wembley. Dalglish would write that people believed it was Liverpool's 'day of judgement', but as the Reds ran out into the sun at Highbury in their grey away kit, it was simply the beginning of a fantastic league season. Dalglish's selection for the opening day was:

> Grobbelaar, Venison, Gillespie, Hansen, Nicol, Johnston, Whelan, McMahon, Barnes, Beardsley, Aldridge.

Expectations were high after Dalglish's Rush-funded spending spree over the summer, but Liverpool would more than repay the faith Dalglish had in his signings – and silence any doubts – with a 2-1 away victory.

The star of the show beyond any shadow of a doubt was John Barnes – as he would so often be that season – running the show from the left flank, and giving Arsenal's new signing Michael Thomas a horrible time at right-back. Liverpool actually started the game somewhat on the back foot but, before ten minutes were gone, their three star signings combined, with Peter Beardsley holding the ball just outside the box and playing a perfectly weighted ball to the overlapping John Barnes, whose cross found John Aldridge to glance the ball into the far corner to make it 1-0 to Liverpool. Brian Moore on commentary called Aldridge a 'lookalike Ian Rush' and, while this may seem unfair, it was a very Rush-like finish to climb above a very capable Arsenal defence and head into the corner.

Unfortunately, less than ten minutes later, Arsenal equalised after Alan Smith knocked a Charlie Nicholas cross into the path of Paul Davis, whose header found the bottom corner from near point-blank range. The match then became a tight affair, with Arsenal's vaunted offside trap frustrating countless Liverpool attacks, though the Reds did have chances to regain the lead. But two minutes from time, the returning Steve Nicol – having suffered a groin injury – scored a quite ridiculous header from the edge of the box after a Barnes free kick had been headed directly into his path by Tony Adams.

Dalglish stated that he was delighted to have started with a win from a tough away game, which is somewhat of an understatement. Highbury remained a tough place to go, and to come away from arguably one of the toughest away games all season with three points demonstrated how capable Dalglish's side were. Morale was high, demonstrated by Craig Johnston's words after the game: 'There's a great atmosphere and a tremendous confidence in the squad. You could tell how much the result meant to us today by the way the coaches were whooping and yelling in the dressing room.' Coming away from London, the only concern was that Peter Beardsley had been taken off after receiving some close attention from the Arsenal defence, Tony Adams in particular, but he would be ready to go next time out.

That would be at Highfield Road against Coventry City. Dalglish named an unchanged line-up, with the manager clearly already confident about his best starting XI. The travelling Liverpudlians – even more making the journey than usual – were obvious in their adoration for the two new signings of Barnes and Beardsley, with Beardsley scoring his first Liverpool goal in a 4-1 victory that Steve Nicol would later claim should have been doubled. Indeed, Nicol himself had a fantastic game, again scoring from left-back, with the other two goals going to the aforementioned Beardsley and John Aldridge. The performance promised much for the rest of the season, with some fantastic flowing, attacking football. Of course, Dalglish made it very clear that he wouldn't be getting carried away. David Lacey in *The Guardian* labelled Liverpool 'reborn'. It's easy to look back now and see it as obvious that this Liverpool side were special, but, just two games in, many of the country's media were quickly noticing that this had the potential to be an all-time great Liverpool side. Even John Sillett, the Coventry manager said, 'We were lucky. It could have been ten.'

Liverpool's last of the three away fixtures came on 5 September, as they suffered their first dropped points of the league season, drawing 1-1 with West Ham United on a wet, poor Upton Park pitch. Dalglish's only change for this game was the introduction of Nigel Spackman on the right wing, with Craig Johnston injured. Spackman would eventually force himself into the side later in the season, but it wouldn't be on the right flank. By all accounts, even including the manager, Liverpool's play on that day more than merited a third consecutive win, but they failed to make their chances pay, and a very rare error by captain Alan Hansen gifted an equaliser to Tony Cottee in the 74th minute, meaning Liverpool would head back to Merseyside unbeaten in the league, but disappointed with the draw.

Nevertheless, Russell Thomas, writing for *The Guardian*, was glowing in his praise for Liverpool, stating: 'To Liverpool's fame, now add a bit more flair. Throw in tactical flexibility – midfield switches at half-time saw West Ham looking even more bemused – and you have the mixture that has champions labelled all around it.' David Prentice for the *Liverpool Echo* labelled Liverpool as 'streets ahead'. Prior to Liverpool's return to Anfield, expectation was more than mounting, both from the fans and the footballing media, and Dalglish's new, rebuilt Reds would have to live up to it.

The Reds finally returned home to Anfield a week later on 12 September, as they faced Aldridge's former team Oxford United. The Anfield faithful – over 42,000 of them – saw an unchanged side, with Johnston still out with a groin injury. It took Liverpool only three minutes to give the home crowd what they wanted, with Barnes's cross setting up Aldridge at the back post to head home and be the scourge of his former side. As Anfield went absolutely wild for Barnes – for the first of many times that season – Ronnie Whelan set the left-winger up to fire home and give Liverpool a two-goal lead only 37 minutes in. Liverpool failed to add to their tally, but this was once again a fantastic performance that pleased the manager, who said of Barnes's performance, 'He did what we expected him to do. He made a goal, scored one, and entertained. You remember that.'

Barnes certainly did entertain, and when Liverpool won 3-2 against Charlton Athletic at Anfield only three days later through goals by Aldridge, Hansen and McMahon, *The Guardian* reported that the Kop 'tingled'. It was the first time that Liverpool had really been challenged so far, with Charlton twice having led, but eventually a classic Liverpool rally saw them take the three points, and move up to third in the table, looking increasingly ominous. Of the result, Dalglish said, 'The lads played some great stuff at times. Some of it in the second half was better than I've seen for a long time.'

Liverpool's next game saw them journey to the North East to face Peter Beardsley's former side Newcastle United in a game shown on the BBC's *Match of the Day*. Newcastle had used £575,000 of the £1.9m from the Beardsley transfer to sign the Brazilian Mirandinha from São Paulo club Palmeiras. Mirandinha has the status of being the first Brazilian to play in England – and comparison with Beardsley was only natural. Any pressure on Beardsley only grew after Mirandinha played well, scoring both goals in Newcastle's 2-2 draw with Manchester United the previous week. Dalglish stuck with the team that finished so well against Charlton in the last game, with Mark Lawrenson coming in to replace Spackman, and Steve Nicol switching from left-back to the right wing.

It was Nicol – or Chico – that stole the show though, scoring a hat-trick as Liverpool blew away Newcastle at St James' Park. His first came fortuitously, as Barnes and Beardsley combined down the Liverpool left, and Barnes's cross rebounded off the Newcastle defender John Anderson directly into the path of Nicol, who easily guided the ball past Gary Kelly in goal. Only seven minutes later, Dalglish's side had their second, as Beardsley and Nicol worked the ball on the right-hand side of the box, and right-back Barry Venison lofted it to Barnes at the back post. His header guided the ball into the six-yard box, where Aldridge stabbed at the ball to score. John Motson on commentary that day for the BBC simply said, 'Liverpool make it look so easy.'

Peter Beardsley more than demonstrated his class in the second half, as he created Liverpool's third goal, and Nicol's second, by running on to a long through ball from Lawrenson at left-back, beating Newcastle's attempted offside trap and squaring the ball across the face of goal for Nicol to finish at near point-blank range. Newcastle got themselves partially back into the game through a penalty by Neil McDonald after Gary Gillespie clumsily brought Mirandinha down, but when Aldridge played a through ball down the right for Nicol to run on to and lift past the keeper in the 70th minute – a goal that would be a candidate for Goal of the Season – the game was finished, and

Liverpool maintained their unbeaten start to the league campaign.

Dalglish was ecstatic with the result and the performance, saying, 'The players must have enjoyed playing but I do not think the opposition could have been too happy. I have said before that it is all about collective involvement and not about individuals.' The result, which the *Liverpool Echo* called a 'masterclass', left Liverpool as the only unbeaten team in the First Division. However, Dalglish stated that Liverpool would not do any more than look ahead to the next game.

That next game was in the League Cup second round, as Liverpool faced Blackburn Rovers in the first leg at Ewood Park. At this point a Second Division side, Blackburn rallied after Steve Nicol opened the scoring after half an hour to level through winger Scott Sellars early in the second half. They headed back to Anfield for the second leg with at least a chance of a giant-killing.

Liverpool closed the month of league competition on 29 September, hosting Derby County on a Tuesday evening in front of over 43,000 at Anfield. Craig Johnston's return to full fitness meant changes for the Reds, as he came back into the side on the right wing, with the surprisingly prolific Steve

Nicol returning to left-back, which meant that Mark Lawrenson was demoted to the bench alongside Paul Walsh. Dalglish's Liverpool faced not only England's starting goalkeeper Peter Shilton that night, but also a five-man defence, clearly a compliment to the fine form in which Liverpool had started the season.

However, the back five could do little to help Derby repel the unstoppable force that was the Liverpool attack, led on this particular night by John Aldridge, who scored his first Liverpool hat-trick. His first was a penalty, converted in the 41st minute after Craig Johnston had been fouled. Liverpool had been denied an opening goal earlier in the half when an indirect free kick from Barnes was ruled to have gone directly in without being touched, but Aldridge's penalty seemed to settle any lingering concerns, and Peter Beardsley made it two in the 47th minute, thanks to work by Aldridge and Johnston. Aldridge converted another penalty in the 68th minute, this time after Barnes had been fouled, then completed his hat-trick as the second half became an 'exhibition', with Johnston setting him up.

Yet more plaudits were heaped on Dalglish's team, with Shilton claiming it was the best Liverpool side he had faced, and the then England manager

Bobby Robson likening the performance of John Barnes to that of George Best. Indeed, Ian Hargraves, writing on the game for the *Liverpool Echo*, said that choosing a man of the match was nearly impossible, but selected Barnes nonetheless. Dalglish stated that he believed it was Liverpool's best display of the season so far, and that even neutrals would have enjoyed their performance. Most importantly, the win and the three points moved Liverpool into second place in the league table, which was described as 'menacing' by the *Liverpool Echo*. If only they had known what was to come.

Chapter 4

Liverpool vs Queens Park Rangers, Saturday, 17 October 1987

Grobbelaar, Venison, Gillespie, Hansen (c), Nicol, Johnston, McMahon, Whelan, Barnes, Aldridge, Beardsley

Substitutes: Walsh, Lawrenson

Referee: Ron Bridges

AS OCTOBER 1987 began, Liverpool sat second in the First Division, three points behind the early pace-setters Queens Park Rangers. Managed by Jim Smith, this was QPR's fifth consecutive season in the top flight, and they had started well, dropping points in only two games all season, playing a back-three system with a sweeper, at that point extremely rare in English football. QPR had held the top spot for the majority of the season so far, but with Liverpool unbeaten and only three points behind – with two games in hand – a win would take Dalglish's side to the top of the table.

Before the showdown against QPR, Liverpool had to face Portsmouth in the league and Blackburn Rovers in the second leg of their League Cup tie. The Reds eased past Alan Ball's Pompey 4-0 at Anfield, with *The Guardian* labelling the game 'a lesson in higher education', and the *Liverpool Echo* calling Dalglish's side the 'red tide'. Next up was the League Cup. After being held 1-1 at Ewood Park, there was no repeat of that feat at Anfield, but it took until the 89th minute for the ever-present John Aldridge to save Liverpool's blushes and put them through to the next round. Arguably, this was the first time Anfield had felt nerves all season, and the game may not have been the best warm-up for the top-of-the-table clash. Despite that, thanks to the international break, Dalglish and Liverpool had 11 days to prepare for the visit of QPR.

After making changes against Blackburn, Dalglish returned to his strongest line-up at this point in the season. Aldridge, in particular, was in a rich vein of goalscoring form, having scored in his last nine Liverpool matches. Over 43,000 were again in attendance at Anfield, with the Kop in full voice, as spare tickets increasingly became a rarity on Merseyside. Demand was so high that the game was sold out a full two and a half weeks beforehand. One face that was certainly recognised in the crowd was that of Ian Rush, who was struggling to settle in and find his goalscoring boots with Juventus.

In the early going, as the Kop sang Rush's name, QPR's plan was clear, with Alan McDonald marking Aldridge, and Paul Parker marking Beardsley. Despite that, Liverpool soon created a chance, with Gillespie playing a fantastic ball from the back up to Beardsley, who laid it off to the onrushing McMahon. His shot, unfortunately, went tamely wide. Aldridge then had his first effort on goal mere minutes later as Liverpool stole the ball from QPR as they attempted to build from the back, and a Beardsley cross found the former Oxford striker, but he was unable to get enough contact on the ball. Liverpool continued to press and harry in midfield as the game became scrappy, but QPR weren't without threat, forcing some good saves from Bruce Grobbelaar in the Liverpool net.

Anfield's first taste of John Barnes for the afternoon came early in the first half. Picking the ball up on the left flank from McMahon, Barnes took on two QPR defenders, somehow managing to keep the ball and go past both of them well after it looked as if he had lost the ball, before playing a dangerous-looking pass into the box that QPR frantically cleared, with McMahon blazing a volley well over the bar. These were early signs, but Barnes would feature heavily as the game progressed.

Seconds later, Liverpool had the ball in the back of the QPR net. Some fantastic defensive work by Beardsley saw him force Kevin Brock off the ball just inside the QPR half, and an excellent through ball found Craig Johnston attacking from the right. His right-footed shot across David Seaman nestled in the bottom corner. Infuriatingly for Liverpool, the official, Ron Bridges, had already blown for a free kick to Liverpool for a foul on Beardsley, meaning the fine goal by Craig Johnston was unfairly chalked off. For several minutes after the decision, Anfield let Ron Bridges know exactly what they thought of his decision. In truth, it was a foul on Beardsley, but the ball had long gone, and the official clearly should have played the advantage to Liverpool with Johnston bearing down on goal.

Johnston eventually got his just reward towards the end of the first half, as John Barnes received the ball just outside the box on the left side of the field. Going past his defender with ease, Barnes reached the byline and fired the ball back across goal, where the right-winger was ready to meet the ball just outside the six-yard box to make it 1-0 to the Reds. John Motson on commentary for the BBC said, 'The Rangers fortress, finally broken.' It was only the sixth goal QPR had conceded all season. As Anfield began to roar, Beardsley had a shot from 20 yards that narrowly missed David Seaman's near post. With the half-time whistle, Liverpool went in at the break 1-0 up.

As the second half began, Liverpool dominated possession, playing towards the Kop, at times passing it around the QPR defence as if they weren't really there. But it was to be a set piece that gave Liverpool a two-goal lead, when John Barnes lofted in a cross from a free kick near the byline, and Ron Bridges judged the ball to have been handled by Dean Coney. Naturally, John Aldridge stepped up, and sent the penalty into the top-right corner, a shot aimed so well that Seaman couldn't reach it, even though he had guessed the right way. The goal marked the tenth game in a row in which Aldridge had scored, as he already led the goalscoring charts in the First Division, and had more than stepped into the role of Ian Rush as Liverpool's primary goalscorer.

At this point John Barnes took over, and the game became a demonstration of his sheer brilliance and undeniable talent. As he began to pick the ball up more in an inside-left position, he increasingly began to put more and more pressure on the QPR backline, and often combined with Beardsley and Whelan. Liverpool began to smell blood and, in the 79th minute, Barnes laid the ball inside to Beardsley just outside of the QPR area. Beardsley played the ball over to the right, with the ball running past Aldridge after an excellent dummy that received an audible roar from the Kop. The resulting cross from Johnston was cleared, but when Ronnie Whelan immediately stole the ball back and played it forwards to Barnes with a deft outside-of-the-foot pass, QPR were scrambling. Barnes then played a beautiful one-two with Aldridge that left him bearing down on goal, and his right-footed shot left Seaman with no chance whatsoever, as it flew into the top corner.

If that goal was good, what Barnes did six minutes later was even better. As QPR moved the ball into midfield, Barnes pressed and as he won the ball from Kevin Brock, it ricocheted forwards. As Barnes ran on to the ball, bearing down on the QPR defence, one defender attempted a sliding tackle to dispossess him, but Barnes simply side-stepped to the left to evade the challenge, before then immediately changing direction to move to his right, taking out both QPR defenders in one single move. Finding himself one on one with David Seaman yet again, another right-footed shot, this time into the bottom corner, gave Liverpool a 4-0 lead, and undoubtedly sealed the game for the Reds. Clearly impressed with Liverpool's performance on commentary, John Motson exclaimed, 'That's a fabulous individual goal,' as Barnes wheeled away, his arm raised in celebration. After the game, Dalglish labelled the goal 'the best I have ever seen at Anfield', and said that Barnes's performance was 'magnificent'. Quite the compliments.

With that, Liverpool had climbed the final step to the top of the table, maintaining their unbeaten start to the league season, and establishing themselves as the team to beat for the remainder of the caampaign. It had been another performance that had validated how Dalglish was asking the team to play, the way he built the team post-Heysel, and the astute signings he had made that had created arguably the most attractive team Liverpool had ever had. Post-match, Aldridge summed the game up quite accurately, saying, 'We just overran them.' Naturally, the media were glowing in their praise for Dalglish's side. David Lacey for *The Guardian* said 'Liverpool will probably win the title,' but it was the quotes given by Ian Rush that were most telling. He said of Barnes, 'He was the best player out there – he's got some skill but he's strong as well.' Rush was also full of praise for the line-up Dalglish had selected, saying, 'And I like the look of Ronnie Whelan and Steve McMahon in midfield. It gives the side a good shape and they are working as a team.' Finally, Phil McNulty for the *Liverpool Echo* said, 'Locked gates and five-star performances are fast becoming an Anfield way of life.'

In truth, although this was quite clearly an incredible performance, completely destroying what was until that point their closest challengers for the title, this wasn't the first time Liverpool had completely blown away their opposition in 1987/88, and it certainly wouldn't be the last. Liverpool were back on top, and it would take an almighty challenge to knock them off.

Chapter 5

Taking Control:
The Rest of October

COMING OUT of the top-of-the-table clash against QPR, Kenny Dalglish's Liverpool had undoubtedly established themselves as the team to beat in English football in 1987/88 – if there had really even been much of a debate to begin with. As if to really hammer home the point to anyone who had any remaining doubt, a day after knocking QPR off the top spot, Dalglish signed midfielder and Republic of Ireland international Ray Houghton from Oxford United for £825,000.

Houghton was the fourth of the five names that Dalglish had given the Liverpool board in the winter of 1986. Having already managed to bag John Aldridge, John Barnes and Peter Beardsley, the right-sided player added the final piece to the seemingly unsolvable puzzle that was the Liverpool team in 1987/88, although Houghton admitted, 'I honestly don't know what I can add to such a great team.' Dalglish had been impressed by Houghton earlier in the season when Liverpool made their first appearance at Anfield following the sewer collapse, soundly beating Oxford 2-0. Dalglish wrote of Houghton, 'I was impressed, and not for the first time, by Ray Houghton's performance in Oxford's midfield. He looks a fine player and is a good competitor.'

However, Houghton's path to Anfield and Merseyside hadn't been an easy one. He was born in Glasgow, but moved to London at the age of ten, and turned professional with West Ham United, signing with them at 17 years of age. However, after only one appearance in three years, he was deemed surplus to requirements by the East End club and moved across London to Second Division Fulham in 1982, where he made 129 appearances, scoring 16 league goals. By 1985, however, he had been signed by Maurice Evans's Oxford, and then began to really demonstrate his talent, helping them to a surprise League Cup success in the 1985/86 season, defeating QPR at Wembley. Incredibly, despite his obvious talent and industry, Houghton hadn't seemed to feature in the plans of the Scotland team, so was snapped up by Republic of Ireland manager Jack Charlton, thanks to Houghton's Irish father. Houghton would go on to have many memorable international moments with the Republic.

Houghton surprisingly went straight into the starting line-up for Liverpool's next game, as they faced Luton Town at Kenilworth Road on their hated artificial pitch. It was Craig Johnston who dropped out, and it was clear that he was disappointed to lose his place so quickly, refusing to comment when asked by the media. Dalglish, however, said: 'I don't see why he should be upset,' and stated that he had an array of attacking talent at his disposal that needed to be used. In truth, Dalglish had spent a total of £4.5m assembling the 1987/88 squad, and he was absolutely going to use it. Johnston wasn't the only established player not to feature at times, with Mark Lawrenson, Jan Mølby and Nigel Spackman also missing out throughout different points of the season.

In the end, Liverpool had Gary Gillespie to thank for heading home the winner in the 70th minute, after a poor first-half performance that suggested Liverpool might be up for another difficult outing on Luton's 'plastic pitch', according to Colin Malam in the *Daily Post*. However, a significantly improved performance after the break meant that, in the end, Liverpool should have won by more than one goal, with Houghton unfortunately failing to score on his debut, being unable to beat goalkeeper Les Sealey in a one-on-one. Nevertheless, even though Luton hit the bar late on, a draw would have been an insulting result for Liverpool, who in the end were more than deserving of the three points as they maintained their momentum, ending the league month sitting top of the First Division, having demonstrated their brilliance for all to see.

However, this wasn't Liverpool's last game of October, as they ended the month with the season's first Merseyside derby, at Anfield, in the League Cup third round. Dalglish made changes for the game, as Craig Johnston and Mark Lawrenson returned to the starting line-up – Ray Houghton was cup-tied and Barry Venison injured – with Liverpool in their standard 4-4-2 shape that they would retain throughout the season. Unfortunately for the red side of Merseyside, Everton produced a fantastic performance on the night, never allowing Liverpool to settle into the style of play they had shown throughout the season so far. Graeme Sharp missed two chances to score before England right-back Gary

Stevens had luck to thank for the winner, his left-footed shot from distance deflecting off the heel of Gary Gillespie and nestling into the bottom corner of the net. Everton gave John Barnes and John Aldridge some pretty close attention throughout the game, with both being sent flying by tackles, but in the end the Blues were deserving of their win, knocking the Reds out of the then Littlewoods Cup.

Naturally, Liverpool would be itching for revenge on their neighbours, and they wouldn't have to wait long to get it. Their next league game was three days later as they again welcomed Colin Harvey's men to Anfield.

Chapter 6

November

AFTER DEFEAT against Everton mere days before in the Littlewood Cup, Liverpool entered November 1987 with quite the point to prove. Incredibly, given their league form and unbeaten start, they also entered the game second in the table behind Arsenal, who had bagged eight straight wins following their opening-day defeat to the Reds. Perhaps to make a deliberate point, Kenny Dalglish made no changes for the game, with Craig Johnston starting on the right flank, and Mark Lawrenson retaining his place in the Liverpool back four. Trevor Brooking on BBC's *Match of the Day* admitted his surprise that £825,000 signing Ray Houghton hadn't been given his home debut for the game, but he did make the bench alongside Jan Mølby. Colin Harvey was forced into changes for the blue half of the city: with Adrian Heath suspended, Wayne Clarke came into the line-up.

For Liverpool, Peter Beardsley started the game alongside the man still firing on all cylinders, John Aldridge. Conversely, Beardsley had come in for some criticism early in the season, with some incredibly saying that Dalglish should have dropped him from the starting line-up. One journalist had even written 'Peter the Plonker', an incredibly unfair and hurtful jibe. Admittedly, Beardsley was taking time to settle at Anfield, and hadn't played his best football yet, with England manager Bobby Robson saying he needed to score more for his club, but any suggestions that the England striker should be dropped were wildly off the mark. Dalglish had taken time to find his own replacement, but he hadn't been wrong in making Beardsley a British record transfer, and he would prove to be more than worth the £1.9m that Liverpool had paid for him.

Liverpool started the derby incredibly brightly, pressing hard and harrying Everton, and forcing an early shot from Beardsley, who found himself in space on the right flank, cutting inside and firing at Neville Southall, but his shot was tame in the end. The first half continued at a pretty frenetic pace, with some tough defending from both sides, including some rough – but sportsmanlike – challenges between Peter Reid and Steve McMahon in the centre of midfield, although minutes later there would be 'words' between Reid and Craig Johnston that demonstrated the real atmosphere of the Merseyside derby. Indeed, when Alan Hansen was reprimanded for a foul on Graeme Sharp later in the first half, the Liverpool captain immediately threw up his arm and let the official Brian Hill know exactly what he thought of the decision.

Minutes later, Liverpool got the breakthrough. After Everton failed to maintain possession from a throw-in, Peter Beardsley managed to stick his foot in and knock the ball towards the middle of the pitch in Everton's half. Immediately moving on to the ball, John Barnes picked it up and had two runners, the aforementioned Beardsley and Steve McMahon, who made a rampaging, penetrating run from midfield. Guiding the ball through the Everton defence with the outside of his skilled left foot, Barnes left McMahon through on goal against Southall and, after what seemed like a moment of hesitation, the midfielder guided the ball over the Everton goalkeeper and into the back of the net. 1-0 Liverpool after 35 minutes. As Anfield roared, McMahon and Aldridge embraced, themselves seemingly roaring along with Anfield. Aldridge raised an arm to the crowd, and the Liverpool bench could be seen celebrating the goal. Dalglish had taken quite the educated gamble in naming an unchanged side, and it appeared to be paying off. As the half-time whistle blew, Liverpool were in the ascendancy, and they would play towards the Kop in the second half.

The Reds began the second period much as they ended the first, with all the momentum. In the opening minutes, Beardsley set Barnes up for a delightful chip that went just wide, but the England winger had been flagged for offside. Beardsley soon received some rough treatment from the Everton backline, challenging for a flick-on by John Barnes and receiving some studs in his side as he tumbled to the Anfield turf. Beardsley almost got his revenge for that challenge by setting up Aldridge, crossing the ball for the forward to tap in from point-blank range, but again the linesman flagged for offside.

Instead, Beardsley would prove his brilliance with a goal of his own, taking the game away from Everton. After Aldridge managed to get his head to a Grobbelaar clearance, Steve McMahon picked up the loose ball and passed to Barnes, who executed a lovely backheel that caused the Kop to audibly roar. McMahon ran on to the backheel and crossed to Aldridge, whose shot ricocheted off Kevin Ratcliffe towards the oncoming Beardsley. Showing incredible technique, Beardsley thundered the ball with his weaker foot on the half-volley, and the ball flew into the back of the net. On commentary, Barry Davies immediately said, 'Beardsley! Oh, that's a lovely goal, that's a lovely goal!' Fans began to rush on to the pitch, one getting so close to Beardsley as to give him a kiss on the cheek.

With no further action in the remainder of the game, Liverpool secured a 2-0 win over their biggest rivals and returned to the top of the table, two points clear of Arsenal with two games in hand. Meanwhile, Everton dropped to seventh. As the teams walked back into the dressing rooms on *Match of the Day*, walking past the famous This is Anfield sign, Barry Davies said poetically, 'Those words continue to say so much to the rest of the teams in the First Division.' With the *Daily Mirror* calling Beardsley's goal 'dazzling', and Harry Harris naming Liverpool's latest performance as another 'televised spectacular', Liverpool had yet again made very clear that nobody in the First Division was currently close to their level.

Liverpool's next game was against the always difficult Wimbledon, and Dalglish named an unchanged line-up for the third straight game, with Ray Houghton still on the bench. However, the Reds weren't at the level they had been against

Everton, and despite a fantastic spell after Houghton came off the bench to give Dalglish's men the lead, Wimbledon pulled Liverpool back, with Carlton Fairweather scoring in the last 15 minutes, meaning the Reds dropped points for only the second time since the league campaign had begun. Despite the draw at Plough Lane, Liverpool returned to the top of the table, with Arsenal continuing to keep the Reds honest.

However, when Liverpool travelled to Old Trafford to face Sir Alex Ferguson's Manchester United – a team that was very much still in the process of a significant rebuild – and drew 1-1, withstanding quite an onslaught from the Manchester side, Liverpool dropped to second in the table. There had been more than a hint of handball in United's equaliser after the incredible John Aldridge had given Liverpool the lead midway through the first half, powering home a header after some terrific work by Steve McMahon. Philip McNulty for the *Liverpool Echo* stated that Liverpool hadn't been at their best, but were fortunate to come up against a Manchester United team who couldn't put Bruce Grobbelaar under any real sustained pressure. In the end, he said, 'Liverpool will be glad to have picked up a point after a lacklustre display.'

Taken together, Liverpool were clearly in their worst run of form all season. Yes, they had remained unbeaten, but two straight draws became three after a 0-0 with Norwich City in front of over 37,000 at Anfield in which Liverpool created plenty of chances but were uncharacteristically profligate with their finishing. As a result of the three straight draws, Liverpool remained second, with Arsenal keeping pace with a fantastic run of wins that had them looking like genuine title challengers, as attractive and dominant as Liverpool had been for the majority of the season thus far. However, it's telling that Stephen Bierley, writing in *The Guardian*, suggested that Watford, Liverpool's next opponnents just three days later at Anfield, were in for quite a difficult time. It does demonstrate the incredibly high standards that Liverpool had maintained throughout their era of dominance over English football that three straight draws had led to rumours of Beardsley being dropped and Dalglish himself returning to the substitutes' bench.

Regardless, over 30,000 at Anfield saw two completely different Liverpool sides face Watford. In the first half, Liverpool were 'lethargic' and 'pedestrian', according to the *Liverpool Echo*, but had John Barnes to thank for waking them out of their slumber, creating the opener for Steve McMahon early in the second half – after the team received a talking-to from Dalglish at the break, which Barnes referred to as a 'kick in the pants' – before goals from Ray Houghton, John Aldridge and Barnes himself secured a 4-0 win that returned Liverpool to the top of the table as Arsenal had lost to Southampton at Highbury. Steve McMahon admitted after the Watford game: 'There was anxiety all around the team in the first half, but once I got the goal you could sense the relief.' Dalglish was a little less happy, saying, 'We were almost like two different sides and I hope the second one is the real Liverpool ... in the first half we were a lot worse than we were on Saturday against Norwich.' Nevertheless, the media in the Merseyside area remained incredibly upbeat about the team despite their relative stutter in form, the *Liverpool Echo* leading with the headline 'Rocket Man!' about Liverpool's star number 10, John Barnes.

Liverpool's final game of November 1987 was an away game. The Reds travelled south to London and White Hart Lane to face Tottenham Hotspur, in a game that was marketed as 'Venables vs Dalglish'. Terry Venables had been Tottenham manager for five days, having returned to England after a very successful period as manager of Barcelona – a stint that only really garnered praise in the latter parts of his career, with one Pep Guardiola talking in positive terms about Venables's impact on the great club. 'El Tel' had taken over Spurs as they languished in mid-table obscurity, with their club hierarchy looking to him to restore the once great club to former glories. Dalglish named a relatively unchanged line-up, although Paul Walsh had to come in to partner John Aldridge up front, with Peter Beardsley out with a knee injury. There had been rumours that Barry Venison would return at right-back, but Dalglish didn't name him in the squad, and instead stuck with Steve Nicol and Mark Lawrenson as his first-choice full-backs. Craig Johnston again found himself on the bench, with Ray Houghton now beginning to stake his claim for the starting spot on the right wing.

The game started evenly, with Liverpool progressing the ball well – especially through Alan Hansen stepping into midfield with the ball – but Tottenham had the best of the early going with two shots on Bruce Grobbelaar's goal that had the Zimbabwean keeper sprawling, only for the attempts to fizz past his posts. Minutes later though, the game changed when England international midfielder Steve Hodge was sent off for swinging an elbow at Ray Houghton as the two tussled for the ball following a Liverpool clearance. Ken Montgomery for the *Sunday Mirror* was hardly sympathetic towards Hodge, writing 'Hodge lets side down' as the headline for his piece on the game, and saying that the England midfielder had 'pulled the mat from under new boss Venables' feet'.

Liverpool certainly took the sending off as an invitation, and turned the screw. Spurs battled bravely against the Reds throughout the first half, with Liverpool being unable to execute the final ball that would break the deadlock. It took until the second half for them to finally take the lead for all of their control, and even then only after Tottenham's keeper Tony Parks had made several excellent saves, including one from Ray Houghton that looked a dead cert to make it 1-0. It was no surprise that Parks was named man of the match.

However, in the 60th minute, Houghton took possession out on the right flank, and he drove forwards – evading a scything Tottenham tackle – to play the ball on to Aldridge on the edge of the box. The top scorer in the league then cushioned the ball across to Steve McMahon, who had made a run forwards from midfield. He simply guided the ball past Parks and into the Tottenham net to make it 1-0. Dalglish then brought on Craig Johnston for Paul

Walsh, who had tried industriously to replace Peter Beardsley, but hadn't been able to recreate the magic that the England striker was capable of on a game-by-game basis. Fortunately, it was the introduced Johnston who gave Liverpool their second, after a deflected cross by Steve Nicol had been skilfully guided on by Aldridge, leaving Johnston with effectively an open net to fire into. With no further goals or action, Liverpool left north London with a 2-0 win, remaining comfortably top of the First Division, with the *Sports Mirror* calling the game simply another 'day at the office' for Liverpool.

As November 1987 ended, Liverpool were sat top of the table, five points clear of Arsenal in second, looking to be coasting through the league campaign, and they remained unbeaten in the league. The club had come through their most difficult period of the season thus far, but remained the team to beat and the clear front-runners for the title. Dalglish's side would head into the final month of 1987 knowing that another good month would see them begin to stretch away from the chasing pack, and put themselves in position for yet another league championship.

Chapter 7

December

AS LIVERPOOL headed towards Christmas 1987, they looked to be in a pretty good position. Dalglish's men were clear at the top of the First Division, with George Graham's Arsenal leading the chasing pack a full five points behind, and with their new signings of John Aldridge, John Barnes, Peter Beardsley and Ray Houghton helping to move Liverpool into what promised to be a brand-new era, but with the same Liverpool dominance over English football. They would play five games throughout the month of December, with three of them being played at the fortress that was Anfield.

On 6 December, over 31,000 at Anfield witnessed Liverpool welcome visitors Chelsea. Not quite the Roman Abramovich-owned club we've come to know in the modern day, but Chelsea were competing in the upper half of mid-table in 1987/88.

Dalglish once again named what was becoming a regular starting XI, with Grobbelaar in goal, and a back four of Lawrenson, Gillespie, Hansen and Nicol. Houghton, McMahon, Whelan and Barnes made up the midfield quartet, with Beardsley floating around behind Aldridge as the front two. Beardsley's ingenuity and creativity had been missed sorely against Tottenham, and his return added significantly to Liverpool's attack. The game itself would be labelled a 'thriller' by the *Daily Post*, as Liverpool would have to come from behind, Mark Lawrenson conceding a penalty in the 22nd minute that was converted by Gordon Durie. Despite that, Liverpool had started brightly, inducing some anxiety in the Chelsea defence, and the Barnes/Nicol combination causing them some issues down Liverpool's left. The Chelsea penalty wasn't the only thing to stop Liverpool's attacking play on the day, as the game had to be halted early in the first half to remove a dog from the Anfield turf. How times have changed.

Nevertheless, Liverpool continued to push forwards, at times the football being quite breathtaking, as Barnes floated infield to combine with McMahon in midfield, and the Liverpool full-backs Lawrenson and Nicol pushing forwards to support the attack. Unfortunately, Liverpool couldn't quite unlock the Chelsea defence, and Aldridge was feeding on scraps despite the lovely combination play in the Liverpool midfield, displaying the 'pass and move' football the club had been so famous for. It was Peter Beardsley, Liverpool's record man, who had the better of the chances in the first half, but both his shots fired just wide of the Chelsea post. There still remained a feeling in December that the Anfield crowd was yet to see the best of Beardsley. By half-time, Liverpool were still 1-0 down, despite their dominance, and Barnes had been followed all half by Clive Wilson, who had put in quite the shift to attack himself, yet track Barnes all over the pitch. In 1987/88, following Barnes like a shadow was sometimes all opposition managers could do tactically to try to stop him.

Liverpool attacked towards the Kop in the second half, and came out with much the same intent they had all season so far – attack in numbers, play it forwards with short, direct passes and score goals. Almost immediately, Aldridge began putting himself about against the Chelsea defence, being penalised for a push seconds into the half, but minutes later he also challenged the Chelsea keeper Roger Freestone for a John Barnes corner, which could have gone anywhere, but unfortunately for the men in red, went wide. Aldridge immediately had some words for the official George Courtney as Chelsea set up for the goal kick. As Anfield became gradually louder and louder, Martin Tyler stated on commentary that 'the second half will be played as much in the mind for Liverpool as in the feet, they mustn't lose their patience'. Minutes later, as Barnes hit the post with a right-footed shot from the edge of the box, those in red on Merseyside must have felt as if the ball would never go in, despite their sheer dominance. Ron Atkinson, joining Tyler as co-commentator, voiced Liverpool's frustration, saying, 'I know when that thing's happening against you, if you're the team that's doing the attacking, you do begin to wonder whether it's not going to be your day.'

Increasingly, Barnes began to find space, floating all over the pitch as the Kop roared louder. The left-winger sent in corner after corner, with none being able to bring the equaliser that Anfield so desperately yearned for. Finally, Hansen managed to find Barnes deep in midfield, and he played a long pass out to Houghton – who had worked tirelessly all game on the right flank. A cross to Aldridge failed to connect, but when the ball was cleared, Ronnie Whelan, showing his immense touch and class immediately controlled it and in the same movement swept his right foot to play the ball out to Steve Nicol on the left flank, moving into the space Barnes had vacated. Hitting the byline after a one-two with Barnes, the Liverpool left-back played it towards the far post, where Peter Beardsley fired home. Infuriatingly, George Courtney immediately blew for a foul by Houghton in the build-up, an incredibly soft push as the ball floated towards Beardsley. Atkinson called the decision 'brave'. David Prentice for the *Daily Post* called it 'curious'. Indeed, one Liverpool fan was reported to have shouted 'go take a bath in acid' at Courtney.

Nicol, getting forwards more and more down the left, created Liverpool's next chance, which was a missed free header by Houghton, as Atkinson's words about it not being Liverpool's day began to look almost prophetic. Liverpool finally got their chance to level when Barnes and Whelan exchanged passes deep in midfield, and the Irish midfielder lofted a beautiful pass over the heads of the Chelsea defence towards the on-running Aldridge, and the league's top scorer was brought down by Joe McLaughlin. The Kop's celebrations were only halted by Aldridge's run-up, as he fired into the top corner, sending Freestone the wrong way and levelling the match after 67 minutes. For the next 20 minutes, Liverpool pushed forwards for the winner, not at all content to settle for the point. Their best opportunity for the winner was actually spoiled by Steve McMahon, with the midfielder playing a far too heavy pass for Ray Houghton as the pair ran through towards a tired Chelsea defence. Fortunately, he would have a chance to reprieve himself minutes later as Houghton, finding himself on the left, played a beautiful one-two with Barnes – with Barnes flicking the ball with his instep – and cut the ball back to a completely unmarked McMahon in the penalty box, who tapped home for Liverpool's second in the 87th minute.

As the Kop applauded as Dalglish's side played out the remainder of the game, it was no less than Liverpool deserved, with Dalglish himself stating as much, saying, 'I think any other result would have been a travesty of justice ... we have not gone behind too often this season. It was something different and they coped superbly well, they showed tremendous depth of character.' John Hollins, the Chelsea boss, promised that Chelsea would win at Stamford Bridge. Undoubtedly, Chelsea had played well, but the Reds had been by far the better side, despite the clear test that the Blues had been. Steven Bierley in *The Guardian* summed it up perfectly, with his summary of the game being titled 'Chelsea sink beneath rising Mersey tide', and he also suggested that snow in Kuala Lumpur was more likely than Liverpool not entering the new year of 1988 top of the First Division, praising the 'invention and verve at Anfield this season'. Still, Liverpool remained five points clear.

However, they would drop points in their next fixture, six days later on 12 December, as they travelled to the south coast to face Southampton at The Dell. Two lovely goals from Barnes gave Dalglish's side a two-goal lead, the first a cushioned volley from an Aldridge cross, and the second a right-footed shot from the edge of the box after a one-two with Beardsley. Unfortunately, Bruce Grobbelaar also had one of his more inconsistent performances, making some great saves but also leaving some watchers scratching their heads with his decision-making, at times having to be saved by his defence, but twice conceding. The first was a looping header that he appeared to have left, but realised too late that the ball was heading in. The second was a shot by Andy Townsend from the edge of the Liverpool box that Grobbelaar couldn't really do much about. Nevertheless, Dalglish was infuriated by what he deemed to be complacency. The manager gave Southampton credit for coming back in the game, but said he was 'disappointed' by the draw. Sadly, Liverpool had also lost Mark Lawrenson, who went off with a hamstring problem. He would be out for a month after starting nine straight games in what had become a very settled back four of Lawrenson, Gillespie, Hansen and Nicol. Sadly, it was the beginning of the end for Lawrenson at Liverpool after what had been a great career.

The draw at Southampton meant that Liverpool were one game away from going 19 league matches unbeaten, equalling a 38-year-old club record from the beginning of a league campaign. They remained five points clear of Arsenal, with a game in hand heading into that potentially record-equalling fixture, welcoming Howard Wilkinson's Sheffield Wednesday to Anfield. Wednesday were down in 17th place but, after going eight games without a win to begin their season, had won five of their last seven games. Liverpool's only change was the return of Barry Venison to the line-up, replacing Lawrenson at right-back. Venison had himself lost his place due to an Achilles tendon injury suffered at Luton back in October, but had at that time been playing extremely well. Prior to the game, Dalglish rubbished any talk of records, and he simply stated, 'We go into every game hoping to avoid defeat.'

The game itself wasn't exactly one of Liverpool's vintage performances in the 1987/88 season, with several reports naming Hansen, Gillespie and Venison as Liverpool's best players on the day, with Beardsley, Houghton and Barnes especially relatively quiet. Wednesday set out to frustrate Liverpool, with Gary Megson used to protect the Sheffield defence and give little room for manoeuvre to the Liverpool attacking line, and Liverpool's usual passing game was disrupted, with Wilkinson's side looking to retain possession themselves as much as possible. Indeed, despite coming away from Anfield with a 1-0 win after Gillespie fired in from point-blank range after a Barnes corner was flicked on by Houghton, the manager stated that Liverpool had played 'within themselves'. When the goalscorer Gillespie was interviewed for television after the game, his goal was phrased as a 'wonderful present'. Perhaps reflecting the attitude of his manager and the club in general, Gillespie said that the players didn't think much of records and that hopefully, come the end of the season in May, they would be league champions, saying, 'You don't win league championships at Christmas, you win them in the summer.' Ian Hargraves for the *Liverpool Echo* wrote that, while the return fixture at Hillsborough on

7 May could cause Liverpool issues '... it will be a major surprise if the championship trophy has not already arrived at Anfield by then'. While the players and staff were remaining laser-focused, the footballing media were clearly aware of just how good this Liverpool side were.

An unchanged side travelled to Oxford on Boxing Day 1987, and those who travelled with them from Merseyside were treated to a fantastic performance, especially from the much-maligned Peter Beardsley, who was at his creative best in a 3-0 Liverpool win. After going close several times in the first half, Liverpool took the lead when Aldridge tapped in a rebound from his own shot against his former club, after a cross from fellow former Oxonian Ray Houghton. John Barnes scored the second as Liverpool executed a classic three versus two counter-attack, with Beardsley having both Barnes and Aldridge to pick from, and expertly laid the ball off to the winger, who fired across the Oxford goalkeeper Peter Hucker and into the net. Steve McMahon made it three with an incredible shot from 25 yards that swerved away from Hucker and into the top corner. Beardsley nearly capped off his incredible performance with a goal, but the post denied him.

The result meant that Liverpool officially broke the club's unbeaten record that stretched back to 1949/50, but more importantly went ten points clear at the top of the First Division, with the bookies making Dalglish's men 8-1 on favourites to win the title. Indeed, Ladbrokes had stopped taking bets on Liverpool winning the First Division. Russell Thomas, writing for *The Guardian*, hinted that Liverpool's football could get even better, as Barnes, Beardsley, Houghton and Aldridge got to know each other better on the pitch, truly a terrifying thought at the time for every manager across England, and especially the chasing pack.

When the Reds demolished Newcastle United 4-0 at Anfield – with goals from McMahon, Aldridge (2) and Houghton – in their final game of 1987, they sat well on their own at the top, a full 16 points ahead of reigning champions Everton, and still unbeaten, having scored over 50 goals in 21 matches. Matt D'Arcy, writing for the *Daily Star*, said, 'Liverpool leave the rest for dead.' At least for the first half of the 1987/88 season, that was undoubtedly correct.

Chapter 8

The Turn of '88, January

AS 1987 bled into 1988, you would have been forgiven as a red on Merseyside for thinking that the First Division was already sewn up. Kenny Dalglish's Liverpool side had been simply peerless through the first half of the season, and had come through the usual tricky Christmas period still remaining unbeaten in league competition.

Over the festive season, the Liverpool captain Alan Hansen was interviewed about the new team he found himself playing for after ten years at the club, and he had some quite revealing remarks about the side, saying, 'The team, I would say, is more attacking than most Liverpool teams I've played in,' and crediting Peter Beardsley and John Barnes for being able to do what most other Liverpool players simply couldn't do from an individual standpoint. Showing his very obvious admiration for the duo, he said, 'It's a pleasure to sit behind them and watch them play.'

Interestingly, from a tactical standpoint, Hansen also linked the £650,000 departure of Graeme Souness to Sampdoria in 1984 to the increased responsibility of the central defenders – Hansen in particular – in building up from the back, saying, 'It's a pleasure now that Graeme Souness left for the centre-backs because when he was playing you could never get a kick, he would just come and take the ball off your feet. Now with Steve McMahon and Ronnie Whelan in the middle, at least you've got a chance of getting a kick.' As understated as the captain was, it was clear how much he was enjoying playing in this Liverpool side, one that attacked relentlessly from the first minute, and had blown teams away in the second half of 1987.

Liverpool began 1988 back in league competition on New Year's Day, as they welcomed Coventry City to Anfield. After his solid return to the side to end 1987, Barry Venison retained his place at right-back, as Dalglish kept faith with the team that had served the red half of Liverpool so well throughout the league season. Like so many others that season, Coventry were swept away by a fantastic Anfield performance, with Peter Beardsley in particular gaining the credit from the footballing media, with his performance being described as a 'champagne show'.

Much of the criticism Beardsley had received in his short Liverpool career had been unfair, but it was clear that he was increasingly settling in at Anfield, and was beginning to put in the kind of performances that the predecessor in his position had been able to on a regular basis. Beardsley opened the scoring in the 22nd minute, before John Aldridge and Ray Houghton increased the lead after half-time, then Beardsley scored his second goal late on. With a 4-0 win, and yet more glorious attacking football, Liverpool moved to a staggering 13 points clear at the top of the First Division, with Brian Clough's Nottingham Forest now appearing to be their closest challengers, and Arsenal, Manchester United, Queens Park Rangers and Everton just behind.

After the game, Coventry's manager John Sillett simply said, 'Nobody will touch them, they are superb.' The scary thing for the rest of English football was former Liverpool goalkeeper Steve Ogrizovic's statement. He said after the game, 'If you try to compare Forest and Liverpool, to me they look a division apart, and I don't think Liverpool were in top gear.' Seemingly everyone, apart from

Dalglish and the Liverpool players, had anointed them champions already, with Michael Henderson writing in *The Guardian*, 'The title race is now merely a canter.' Henderson even compared the flair and style of Dalglish's side to the great Dutch teams of the 1970s. If you asked many on Merseyside who watched the great 1987/88 side, they would likely echo that statement.

Days later, on 4 January, the club agreed a deal that would see John Wark leave, as he headed back to Ipswich Town for £100,000. Wark later said, 'Hard as it was to depart Anfield, I knew it was the right thing to do.' Wark had lost his place with the emergence of Jan Mølby, and, following the advice of Bobby Robson, chose to return to the Second Division club.

Liverpool now took a break from their dominance over the First Division, to instead focus on the FA Cup. In the third round, they faced Stoke City, then of the Second Division. Dalglish – as was customary in those days – named a full-strength side to face the Potters, with Mark Lawrenson making his return from injury at full-back. On a cold, wet and muddy day at the Victoria Ground, the league leaders were incredibly held to a draw by their second-flight opponents, with Vince Wilson for the *Sunday*

Mirror arguing that Stoke should have actually won the game, with misses by Simon Stainrod and Steve Parkin costing Stoke a quite incredible cup upset. They even had a gilt-edged opportunity in the final minute, but substitute Graham Shaw snatched at his chance when one on one with Mike Hooper. In the end, Liverpool might well have been happy with the draw, with Hooper, chosen in goal due to a training injury to Bruce Grobbelaar, saying, 'I'm happy to have kept a clean sheet and relieved to get a draw.' Nevertheless, Stoke's fantastic performance gained them a replay three days later, in front of nearly 40,000 spectators at Anfield.

In what was a tried and tested Dalglish move, the Liverpool manager stuck with his line-up from the previous game, with Mark Lawrenson retaining his place in the back four. Again, Stoke performed admirably, with Ian Ross in *The Times* writing, 'The Potteries side bowed out of the cup with their pride intact after a display of raw courage.' Indeed, Liverpool were possibly quite fortunate to get through to the next round. Once again, Stoke had chances and looked dangerous on the counter, but failed to put them away. Despite Stoke's effort, Liverpool's quality quickly shone through, with Peter Beardsley scoring after only eight minutes to give Liverpool the lead, and despite mounting strong attacks through the remainder of the game and looking to extend their lead, they were unable to score a second. Fortunately for those in red on Merseyside, Liverpool's performance was far better than it had been three days earlier, with *The Times* reporting, 'Liverpool played with such effortless ease that it was difficult to understand exactly how Stoke had managed to hold them in check.' Liverpool's reward was a fourth-round tie at Second Division side Aston Villa, travelling to Villa Park at the end of January.

However, attentions on Merseyside quickly turned to Liverpool's next fixture. On 16 January, they returned to league competition, as they looked to continue their seemingly unstoppable march towards the First Division title. They faced George Graham's Arsenal, who had still maintained somewhat of a title challenge, but knew they needed to beat Liverpool to stand any chance of catching Dalglish's men, with the Reds 14 points ahead. The game was one of the great Liverpool performances that season.

Chapter 9

Liverpool vs Arsenal, Saturday, 16 January 1988

Hooper, Lawrenson, Gillespie, Hansen (c), Nicol, Houghton, McMahon, Whelan, Barnes, Aldridge, Beardsley

Substitutes: Johnston, Spackman

Referee: Keren P.J. Barratt

LIVERPOOL'S RETURN fixture against Arsenal on 16 January was yet another opportunity for Dalglish's side to display their dominance over everyone else in the First Division in the 1987/88 season. The game was shown by the BBC on *Match of the Day*, but in a demonstration of the drawing power that this Liverpool side had, both domestically and internationally, the game was expected to be the most watched league fixture in the history of English football, and the game was shown in 50 countries all over the globe, with Jan Mølby working for Danish television for the game, and the great Michel Platini in attendance at Anfield for French television. The match was completely sold out, with even star player John Barnes being unable to buy two tickets the day before the game. Such was the appeal of Liverpool in 1987/88 that this was expected to be a showcase of how British, English football in particular, had improved after the hooliganism problems of the decade, and Heysel.

Dalglish stuck with his most trusted selection, as Mark Lawrenson retained his place at right-back, which was the position that had seen most competition all season, and Ray Houghton continuing to be selected on the right flank ahead of Craig Johnston. George Graham, looking to be the first Arsenal manager to win at Anfield since 1974/75, chose to go big against Liverpool's back four, with both Niall Quinn and Alan Smith selected to physically challenge Gary Gillespie and Alan Hansen, the duo that had been so solid all season in what was an incredibly attacking Liverpool side.

Liverpool began strongly on the attack, and Ronnie Whelan's industry created their first chance, as his lofted ball into the box from the left channel fell to Steve McMahon after a poor clearance by Gus Caesar. Unfortunately, McMahon's shot was blocked. As so often that season, Liverpool began on the front foot, and immediately had the Arsenal defence on their heels as the Kop roared into life, recognising the attacking flair of Dalglish's side. John Motson on commentary for the BBC summed it up perfectly, saying, 'Everybody on the Kop, so excited by this prolific Liverpool run … so much interest renewed in football this season, and nowhere more than here.' As English football began to recover its reputation in the late 1980s, it was clear that Liverpool Football Club were at the forefront of that movement.

From the resulting corner and combination play by Barnes and Nicol on the left flank, Arsenal quickly cleared, but it was plain to see that the game wasn't going to be an easy afternoon for the – somewhat in the future – much-vaunted Arsenal back four. Mere seconds later, Liverpool had their second shot of the game as Houghton, Whelan, Barnes and Beardsley raced towards the Arsenal box after a long ball by Lawrenson towards Aldridge. However, Dalglish's second signing from Oxford blazed the ball well wide from 25 yards. Liverpool won the ball following the goal kick by John Lukic, though, and quickly launched into a dangerous attack, with

Barnes playing the ball straight through the Arsenal midfield to Beardsley, who executed a delightful one-two with Aldridge before playing McMahon into space. Unfortunately, the midfielder's touch deserted him, and the ball found its way back to Lukic. The move was a perfect example of the 'pass and move' football that had become so influential across English football, but had its roots in the Boot Room in the days of Bill Shankly.

Arsenal finally found themselves in the Liverpool third after John Barnes was caught in possession, with Alan Hansen, who had a fantastic first half, forced to step in to tackle Alan Smith as he bore down on the Liverpool penalty area. From the resulting throw, Liverpool faced a cross from Nigel Winterburn that was cleared, but only as far as former Everton player Kevin Richardson, whose shot forced Mike Hooper, still standing in for the injured Bruce Grobbelaar, to make a save down to his right at full stretch.

Minutes later, with Liverpool back in possession, they found themselves again bearing down on the Arsenal goal. After a Liverpool throw-in found its way to Alan Hansen, the captain played a wonderful pass forwards through the lines to Aldridge, who played a lovely little flick round the corner to the on-running Steve McMahon. In a two-on-one situation

against the Arsenal defence, McMahon flicked it
to the right to Ray Houghton, but McMahon's pass
ricocheted off the Liverpool number nine and into
the clutches of Lukic. In sheer admiration, John
Motson said, 'Well, some of the football Liverpool
have played this season, typified by that last move.'

However, Arsenal continued to press and harry
Liverpool as the first half progressed, demonstrating
why many had tipped them as title challengers for
1987/88, with central defender Tony Adams even
having a good chance fall to him following a throw-
in, but his first-time volley went wide of the Liverpool
goal. Arsenal seemed content to go very direct, often
pumping long balls from Lukic directly into their
front two of Smith and Quinn. On the counter
Arsenal looked dangerous, with another shot, this
time from Niall Quinn, careering off the leg of Steve
Nicol and going just wide of the Liverpool goal for a
corner. As half-time approached, if anything Arsenal
had the better of the chances, but when Liverpool had
been able to progress the ball through midfield, they
looked constantly dangerous, just lacking that final
moment of quality to score. Arsenal's players were
clearly looking to get to half-time as Liverpool began
to press forwards, with Gus Caesar being spotted by
John Motson asking the official how long remained

until half-time. Arsenal had definitely defended well, with Ken Montgomery for the *Daily Mirror* calling their efforts 'heroic'.

With one minute remaining in the half, Alan Hansen once again progressed the ball through midfield, finding Peter Beardsley, who laid it back to John Barnes. Barnes played a first-touch pass into the path of Steve Nicol, marauding forwards from left-back. Shaping to take on Nigel Winterburn, Nicol instead laid the ball perfectly into the path of Barnes, who had turned and made a run after himself playing Nicol into space. Bursting into the penalty area, Barnes slalomed through the Arsenal defence, with the *Daily Mirror* describing his movement as like an 'eel'. As Kenny Samson came to challenge Barnes at the byline, the left-winger played it across the face of goal, with Ray Houghton somehow failing to convert the ball as it flew past him. McMahon, following up, fired the ball back towards goal but, following a Tony Adams block, Arsenal cleared the ball towards touch, seemingly wanting the ball anywhere but near their goal, and now desperate to hear the half-time whistle.

As the ball trickled towards the touchline, McMahon sprinted after it, and after an incredible run, put his foot on the ball to stop it going out.

Unfortunately, he nearly careered into the Anfield crowd in the process. Turning round and going back for the ball though, he somehow managed to get back to it ahead of a sliding Arsenal foot, moving the ball to the side with incredible ease to keep it in play. As Arsenal began to scramble, McMahon played the ball inside to Beardsley, who was moving into the box. Liverpool's record signing then played the ball across goal, where Lukic could only get a hand to it, knocking the ball towards the back post where it found John Aldridge, who slid in to score his 20th goal of the season to give Liverpool the lead on the stroke of half-time. As the Kop roared, Ronnie Whelan embraced Steve McMahon, who rightfully was given his flowers by John Motson, who said, 'What about McMahon's contribution there? Absolutely fantastic. No wonder they're shaking his hand.' It was a goal that only Liverpool could score, a mix of creativity, skill, ingenuity, graft and timing. As Anfield erupted with chants of 'Liverpool, Liverpool, Liverpool', the half-time whistle blew, and despite putting in one of the best performances of any visiting team at Anfield throughout the 1987/88 season so far, Arsenal found themselves behind at half-time.

When the Gunners came out for the second half, they had been forced into a change, bringing on youngster Michael Thomas for Gus Caesar, who had gone off injured. Caesar had played a significant role in Liverpool's opener, being unable to stop John Barnes as he had scythed through the Arsenal backline. As the ball pinballed between both sides in the opening minutes of the second half, Arsenal actually had one of the better open-play chances all game, when Kevin Richardson played a ball down the left flank for Martin Hayes. Hayes played it across the Liverpool box in front of the Kop, but fortunately David Rocastle's shot at the back post was tame, and the ball trickled towards Alan Hansen, who cleared. Liverpool were fortunate that Hansen's positioning had been so good, though, as Hooper had been well beaten by the shot, and only its lack of speed stopped Arsenal from grabbing a vital equaliser, in what was clearly an uphill battle to come back at Anfield. Indeed, John Motson had implied that it was easier to make a comeback at Wembley than it was against Liverpool at the fortress that was Anfield in the 1980s. Nevertheless, George Graham's side continued with their direct approach towards Smith and Quinn, which did have some success despite the scoreline.

In the 51st minute, one such occasion saw an Arsenal flick-on reach Mark Lawrenson, and uncharacteristically the Liverpool right-back leathered the ball out of play to the surprise of Anfield and the commentators. Immediately, Liverpool made a change, with Nigel Spackman coming on in Lawrenson's place, with the Republic of Ireland international going off, shaking his head as he was consoled by Roy Evans. Lawrenson had nursed an injury throughout the game, and had struggled in recent weeks. It would turn out to be his final game for the club, as his injury problems brought a premature end to his career. Lawrenson had done well to compete with the younger Barry Venison for the right-back spot, but admitted that he wasn't the player he had once been, with wear and tear starting to impact him. Lawrenson said, speaking to the *Sunday Mirror*:

> None of the other Liverpool players in the Liverpool side had any idea how badly I was struggling. They were playing so well and winning, that their performances masked my weaknesses. When I got back into the team, I found I couldn't turn and run like I used to be able to do. I was just getting by on my positional play and my experience. I found I was a yard slower than everyone else and I couldn't get away with it against top-

class teams. When Arsenal's Martin Hayes beat me to the ball over 20 yards twice in a minute, I looked at the bench and knew it was time to pack it in. It came as a complete bombshell to Kenny Dalglish. When the surgeon and I told him, he was speechless. I just couldn't run at all. My Achilles is two and a half times bigger in my right leg now.

I had an operation and carried on playing for 16 months but I was an impostor. I had lost all of my pace and couldn't put myself about.

Without doubt, Lawrenson had been a fantastic player in his seven years at the club, excelling in multiple positions across the pitch, and despite his statements about the decline in his play following his first Achilles injury, it must be said that when he played in 1987/88 he at no point brought the level of the team down, and played very well at right-back. His absence was a problem that Dalglish had to solve.

Still Arsenal continued to pump the ball long against the Liverpool defence, but still the defence held firm, this time Gary Gillespie managing to force the ball forwards to Peter Beardsley, who had very much started coming into form in the famous red shirt. As he ran at the Arsenal defence, he fired a left-foot shot that sent John Lukic scrambling, the keeper only just managing to get a hand on it to stop it nestling into the bottom corner of the goal. The resulting corner unfortunately came to nothing, but Beardsley's aggressive dribbling at the Arsenal defence promised much for the remainder of the game. Liverpool should perhaps have made it two only seconds later when a sloppy pass by Tony Adams allowed Ronnie Whelan to slip John Aldridge in, but his hard shot was saved by Lukic, who kept Arsenal in the game.

Increasingly, Liverpool took control. The ball continued to pinball from Arsenal to Liverpool, but it always seemed to find its way back to a red shirt. As the ball found Nigel Spackman, deputising at right-back, he fired a left-footed pass down the right channel to Aldridge, who deftly laid the ball off to Whelan, who guided it inside to Beardsley. Around 25 yards from goal and in space, he began to run at the Arsenal defence, with Michael Thomas moving to close him down. As the Arsenal substitute came towards him, Beardsley beautifully nudged the ball through the legs of his sliding challenge, and expertly lofted it over a sprawling Lukic and into the back of the net. As Anfield erupted, John Motson made two statements, the first, 'Oh, brilliantly done by Peter

Beardsley,' the second, 'A goal designed to bring any ground to its feet … what can you say apart from pure genius.'

Motson's admiration for this side was evident each time he commentated on a Liverpool game in 1987/88. Of all the incredible goals Liverpool scored that season, it ranks up there with Barnes's double against Queens Park Rangers back in October for sheer individual brilliance. The *Sports Mirror* called it a 'wonder goal', and Norman Wynne in the *Daily Express* called it 'one in a million'. Anfield certainly agreed, as they belted out 'there's only one Peter Beardsley'. He had been so often criticised for his performances earlier in the season, but he had more than proven in this game that he was every bit the player that Dalglish had believed him to be when he paid Newcastle United £1.9m for his services.

Liverpool then began to turn on the style. With the game in hand and any nerves disappearing, they pushed forwards, urged on by the Anfield crowd. John Barnes came infield more often, and Steve McMahon started to get forwards again. Arsenal's frustration also became clear, as their treatment of Liverpool became more physical. In effect, this defeat would mark the end of any remaining hopes Arsenal had of a title challenge in 1987/88, and it was obvious. Just to rub salt in the Gunners' wounds, the Kop began to chant 'champions'. It was hard to disagree with their assessment of the league season. As if to exacerbate Arsenal's fury, they hit the post just minutes later, Niall Quinn heading a Nigel Winterburn cross into the upright. As the remaining minutes ticked away, John Motson genuinely questioned how this Liverpool team were going to be beaten, and whether they would achieve a century of league goals.

As the final whistle went, Liverpool were still harrying and pressing Arsenal, forcing them into back-passes and sloppy passes between the midfield and the back four. With their 23rd unbeaten game, Dalglish's side had emphatically demonstrated their dominance once again. As the undoubted player of the match, John Motson gave Peter Beardsley perhaps the ultimate compliment by comparing his performance to that of a certain other famous Liverpool number seven. It was the striker's birthday the following Monday, and I'm sure that plenty on Merseyside would have been happy to buy him a present after a simply incredible performance. Even Dalglish lavished praise on Beardsley, saying, 'A great goal. You've got to stand up and pay tribute to somebody who scores a goal like that.'

In front of the aforementioned worldwide television audience, it was a perfect example of what English football could be at its very best, and what Liverpool Football Club could be. David Lacey in *The Guardian* wrote, 'Liverpool players deserve a European stage,' making the point that Liverpool should not have continued to be punished for the horrific events at Heysel in 1985, and that this Liverpool team was so good that it deserved to compete with the Real Madrids and Napolis of Europe. The Football Association had made a plea to UEFA's executive committee in Monaco to allow English teams to return to European competition, but without much hope of success. Michel Platini said after the game, 'They have some superb individuals, and I particularly enjoy the way they play to feet. Everyone would like to see them back.' Irrespective of Heysel, the argument that the 1987/88 Liverpool side was good enough to challenge in Europe is without doubt, and it remains a great shame to this day that they were never able to do so during their prime.

Chapter 10

Dominance, the Rest of January

FOLLOWING THE incredible 2-0 victory over Arsenal at Anfield on 16 January, Liverpool moved a full 15 points clear at the top of the First Division. The outlook was rosy at Anfield, including the club announcing a new sponsorship deal with Italian domestic appliance company Candy. Liverpool signed a £1 million deal spread over three years with the Italian brand, another example that the club was beginning to recover its reputation across Europe, along with English football in general. Captain Alan Hansen, John Aldridge, Ronnie Whelan, John Barnes, Ray Houghton and Peter Beardsley took part in promotional shoots sporting the new sponsor over the iconic Adidas-manufactured red Liverpool shirt. David Ost, the managing director of Candy said, 'The new relationship with its Merseyside and Italian links is extremely positive. Great credit must go to

Liverpool and Juventus for the great strides they have made to build bridges between the nations following the tragedy of Brussels. This gives us all the chance to further complete that bridge-building process.'

John Smith, the Liverpool chairman, paid credit to the loyalty Crown Paints showed the club, having sponsored Liverpool for six years, and continuing to sponsor the club despite the bad publicity they received as a result of the Heysel disaster. Candy would sponsor Liverpool from the beginning of 1988/89, as the club continued to go through its healing process.

Back in league action a week after the win against Arsenal, Dalglish's side travelled south to London to face Charlton, who were in the midst of a difficult season, sitting right at the bottom of the table and fighting to remain in the First Division. With Mark Lawrenson out, never to return, Barry Venison returned to the starting XI to play right-back. Other than that, the selection remained Dalglish's preferred starting line-up that season, with Gillespie, Hansen and Nicol making up the rest of the back four, Houghton, Barnes, McMahon and Whelan making up the midfield quartet, and Beardsley and Aldridge ever-present up front as the striking two. Mike Hooper continued to deputise for

Bruce Grobbelaar, who was still unavailable after the gashed leg he'd suffered. With 28,000 in attendance, it was nearly four times the usual attendance at Charlton home games. This Liverpool side were big box office, and it wasn't just at Anfield where tickets were nearly impossible to come by. Everyone across England wanted to see them. David Lacey, writing for *The Guardian* regarding Bob Paisley's statement that Liverpool were leading the weakest First Division he could recall, stated, 'What cannot be in doubt is the hold Liverpool have taken on the English footballing public this season. Television has captured many of the marvellous pieces of individual skill produced, principally, by Barnes and Beardsley this season, and as a result the fans have flocked to see them in the flesh.'

Incredibly, given their recent form, Liverpool looked shaky early on at Selhurst Park, and Charlton had the better of the early chances. However, as the first half developed, Liverpool gained control. Steve Nicol missed perhaps the best chance they created in the first half when he played a one-two with McMahon from a corner and fired just wide as he raced into the box. Fortunately for Nicol, it didn't matter, as minutes later John Barnes's twisting and turning led to his deflected cross falling directly into the path of the in-form Peter Beardsley, whose left-footed shot flew straight past Charlton goalkeeper Bob Bolder and into the net. Liverpool made it two in the second half, when man-of-the-match Barnes received a lay-off from Ray Houghton, who had marched through midfield and was bearing down on the Charlton defence, and side-stepped Bolder to finish effortlessly.

It was yet another example of Barnes's brilliance in a season full of them, and he wasn't even close to being done. Neither were Liverpool. Dalglish's men were 17 points clear now at the top of the table. They were also only five matches away from equalling the 1973/74 Leeds United side's record of going 29 league matches unbeaten from the start of a campaign, and many in the footballing media felt that it was only a matter of time before they either equalled or bettered that record.

The red side of Merseyside closed January 1988 in FA Cup action, as they faced Aston Villa at Villa Park on 31 January. Bruce Grobbelaar made his awaited return to the starting XI in goal, and an injury to Gary Gillespie forced a change in the back four, as Steve Nicol was shifted inside to partner Alan Hansen at centre-back, Gary Ablett coming in at left-back. Injury to Ronnie Whelan, who had been fantastic all season, forced another change, as Nigel Spackman came in to replace him in midfield, in what looked like a patchwork quilt of a Liverpool line-up.

Nevertheless, Graham Taylor's Aston Villa, flying high at the top of the Second Division, made life difficult for Dalglish's side, with plenty of quick attacks and direct running in the first 15 minutes that saw several corners for the home side. Villa Park was loud throughout the match, giving the Aston Villa players plenty of support, and it clearly gave Graham Taylor's side bags of energy, as they certainly gave a good account of themselves against what was evidently the best team in the country *by far*. Towards the latter portion of the first half, Liverpool really took control of the game as Villa lost momentum, and never really let up. Beardsley forced a fantastic save from Nigel Spink in the Villa goal, and John Aldridge – who had just verbally committed to Liverpool through the media amid interest from Sampdoria – hit the bar before the end of the first half as Liverpool went in at half-time level at 0-0, but it was clearly a matter of time.

As the second half began, Liverpool picked up a free kick just inside the Villa half. Taken by Nicol, he played the ball towards Gary Ablett, who flicked into the box. The ball headed towards Aldridge, who turned and executed an overhead kick that saw the ball sail well over Spink and towards the Villa net, but somehow found only the bar to keep the shot out. Minutes later, though, Liverpool had the breakthrough. Nicol, playing fantastically at centre-back in a position he had never played before in a senior game, played the ball down the right flank towards Beardsley, who effortlessly guided it towards the sprinting Ray Houghton with his head. As the right-winger ran on to the ball, he crossed towards the back post, where the mercurial John Barnes was on hand to head back towards goal, the ball nestling in the bottom corner. It was a fantastic team goal, yet it doesn't even rank in the top-ten goals scored by Liverpool that season.

Villa continued to push and forced some fine saves out of Bruce Grobbelaar, who more than justified his immediate return to the line-up after the fine performances of Mike Hooper, but in the final minutes of the game Ray Houghton received the ball on the right wing and played it inside to the underlapping Barry Venison. He played the ball forwards to Aldridge, who made the run into the channel he was so skilled at. As the league's top scorer cut the ball back towards the penalty area,

Peter Beardsley met the ball and fired it into the bottom corner with his weaker left foot, securing Liverpool's progress to the FA Cup fifth round. Philip McNulty wrote 'Blockbusters' in the *Liverpool Echo* and called the team the 'Super Reds'. David Lacey in *The Guardian* was full of admiration for Dalglish's side, praising Nicol's performance at centre-back. The manager dealt out plenty of praise for the side, also giving Nicol credit for his performance, but also gave Nigel Spackman his flowers for stepping into the side almost unnoticed. Dalglish said, 'It was a well-deserved win. We had good performances right throughout the team.'

The win was also Liverpool's ninth consecutive clean sheet, as they continued to march on, seemingly sweeping the rest of English football aside. The club ended January 1988 a full 17 points clear at the top of the First Division, and through to the FA Cup fifth round. It looked as if Liverpool could win everything they wanted to, in whatever manner they desired. The control Dalglish's side now had over the 1987/88 league season was incredible, and they had plenty still left in the tank.

Chapter 11

February

AS FEBRUARY 1988 began, Liverpool Football Club appeared to be strolling towards yet another league championship. Having dominated the league through the first portion of the season, Kenny Dalglish's side now faced the task of finishing off the job they had started back in August, and maintaining the incredibly high standards they had achieved in countless performances both at Anfield and on the road.

Their first game of February was at Anfield, as they welcomed John Lyall's West Ham United to the stadium that had been nothing short of a fortress in 1987/88. Dalglish continued with the system and the shape that had served the team so well throughout the season, and chose the same line-up as he had in the FA Cup against Aston Villa, with Steve Nicol continuing alongside captain Alan Hansen in central defence, and Nigel Spackman partnering Steve McMahon in what may have been a less creative midfield without Ronnie Whelan, but was an all-action, combative one. Hardly anyone who turned up at Anfield on 6 February would have had much hope for the London side, with Liverpool at the peak of their powers.

However, Liverpool found themselves frustrated all afternoon by West Ham, with John Lyall's side putting up dogged resistance, closing the opposition down throughout the game, and setting up in a more solid defensive shape than many visitors to Anfield had that season. Perhaps the most incredible moment of the game came early in the first half when Peter Beardsley beat his marker down the byline, and cut the ball back towards the six-yard box. The ball then deflected off a West Ham heel and fell into the path of John Barnes, who fired his shot low and hard. Somehow the ball bounced up off the Anfield turf and caught a flailing leg to send it flying over the bar. Barnes had further efforts throughout the game, but all were well saved by the West Ham goalkeeper Tom McAllister. Ultimately, despite all their possession and passing football, Liverpool were unable to get the ball over the line, aside from Peter Beardsley's deft chip over McAllister from eight yards out, but only after John Aldridge had dragged down Gary Strodder following a long ball by Ray Houghton. In the end, the game finished 0-0, only the second time all season that Liverpool had failed to score. However, their unbeaten run continued, as they closed in on Leeds' record.

The *Liverpool Echo* called the game the 'Hammer Hold', but David Lacey in *The Guardian* was perhaps more accurate, stating that with Nicol playing at centre-back due to the absence of Gillespie and Lawrenson, Liverpool had lacked the attacking thrust they had so often received from their full-backs, and Nicol in particular, who so often had overlapped and underlapped and dovetailed expertly with Barnes in 1987/88. Dalglish accepted the result but said, 'If an early chance had gone in it would have been a different ball game.'

Liverpool's next game was again in league action, as they faced another side from the London area, but this time travelled south to play the struggling Watford. This would be the first time John Barnes had faced the Hornets at Vicarage Road since his £900,000 transfer in the summer. To describe the pitch at Vicarage Road as a quagmire would be doing a disservice to quagmires, and it certainly wasn't the kind of playing surface that suited Liverpool's much-vaunted 'pass and move' playing style. The manager once again named an unchanged line-up, with Liverpool still without the crucial Gary Gillespie, who had been missed significantly in the back four.

Liverpool's ability to maintain their style on such a pitch demonstrates the technical capability that existed in the side, but Dalglish's team were also plenty able to put themselves about and challenge Watford for the classic 50/50 balls that such a pitch created. Barnes was booed and jeered every time he picked up the ball, but he doggedly continued, dribbling aggressively and directly at the Watford defence. Liverpool did have moments of worry though, including a classic moment of Bruce Grobbelaar goalkeeping, where he came out to claim a Watford corner – after a fantastic save – but flapped at the ball, leaving it up for grabs around the penalty area, but Watford blazed it over the bar.

Nevertheless, Liverpool almost scored through Aldridge, who fluffed a chance he really should have scored after a flick-on by Barnes – although the pitch provided a pretty good excuse – before they opened the scoring through Beardsley, who picked the ball up from Nigel Spackman just outside of the box, beat his man and fired low and hard across goal to make it 1-0. Beardsley was beginning to get the recognition he had deserved all season, not just in England, but across Europe too. Prior to the game, Beardsley had stated, 'I'll never want to go abroad,' as rumours about a transfer swirled. Rudi Völler, then in his first season at Roma, had talked about both Barnes and Beardsley, calling them 'world class', and saying, 'I can understand why Gary Lineker scores so many goals for England when I see the service he gets from Barnes and Beardsley.' The German forward also said, 'It is a pity that Liverpool cannot play in Europe. It would be great to play against them.'

With the opener scored, Liverpool hit their stride. Barnes had a fantastic opportunity that he toe-poked just side, and although they had to wait until after half-time, they scored their second only two minutes into the second half when Ray Houghton squared for the unstoppable John Aldridge, who scored his 21st goal of the season. Beardsley scored his second of the game in the 49th minute, as he picked the ball up just inside the box, rounding a Watford defender and the goalkeeper before calmly side-footing the ball into the back of the net. Barnes gained a modicum of revenge for the jeering he received when he scored Liverpool's fourth, firing home a John Aldridge knock-down from a Barry Venison cross.

Ken Montgomery in the *Daily Mirror* wrote 'Peter the Great', clearly giving Beardsley the credit for an incredible performance. Indeed, much of the footballing media was salivating at the prospect of Barnes and Beardsley invigorating Sir Bobby Robson's England squad, who would face Israel in midweek. *The Guardian* suggested that the Liverpool duo were the answer to what was called 'England's jigsaw puzzle'.

Two days later, on 15 February, Paul Walsh was sold to Terry Venables's Tottenham for £500,000. After a much-rumoured falling-out with Dalglish, involving some choice words being thrown at Dalglish by Walsh, and after falling further out of favour following the signing of Peter Beardsley, Walsh had found himself relegated to the substitutes' bench at best. What had once appeared to be an incredibly promising career at Anfield turned out to be a 'what if' of England football. Regardless, Liverpool were too busy on their march towards the championship for Walsh's departure to have any impact. Their next game was a big one, the 162nd Merseyside derby, at Goodison Park in the FA Cup fifth round.

Once again, Dalglish selected the same line-up he had for the previous month, with Nicol at centre-back, and Venison and Ablett as the full-backs. Nicol's performances had been so impressive throughout the 1987/88 season that the *Daily Star* had Nicol voted as being the best defender in the country that season, ahead of Manchester United's Paul McGrath. The man he was deputising for at the time, Gary Gillespie, was placed third. Also of note was the top three clean-up Liverpool scored in the voting for midfielders, with Steve McMahon, Ronnie Whelan and Craig Johnston being rated first, second and third, respectively.

BBC had the coverage for the game on *Match of the Day*, and opened the coverage by saying, 'Is there anywhere better for a football enthusiast to be this afternoon, than at Goodison Park?' Although Colin Harvey's Everton had lagged significantly behind their neighbours across Stanley Park in 1987/88, the game remained must-see television. Alongside Jimmy Hill in the studio, Tottenham manager Terry Venables spoke in glowing terms about several of the Liverpool players, particularly McMahon, Beardsley and Barnes.

As the game kicked off, John Motson on commentary was as always full of praise for football on Merseyside, and credited the fans of both teams for creating an atmosphere that rivalled football anywhere on the planet. As expected from a Merseyside derby, the first minutes in particular saw the football changing possession multiple times, and some tough tackling from both teams. The footballing pinball ended with the first real attempt at goal, as Everton worked the ball towards Trevor Steven, just inside the Liverpool box, but his shot was easily saved by Bruce Grobbelaar. Liverpool immediately attacked from Grobbelaar's distribution and won a corner through Barnes, who immediately received loud boos from the Goodison crowd. Barnes received far worse that day, and an infamous photo was captured that showed Barnes having to backheel away a banana that had been thrown at him by a member of the crowd. Everton chairman Philip Carter later labelled the fans involved as 'scum'.

The Goodison crowd continued to roar loudly for the men in blue, as Adrian Heath had another shot on goal, in the end a tame effort that he should have done better with. The ball into the box that created the chance had been from Everton captain Peter Reid, who had already been off the field for treatment. Reid collapsed in pain following the cross, and Harvey was forced to take him off, replaced by Paul Bracewell. Liverpool continued to fight, scratch and claw, but without much to show for it in terms of attacking threat, save for John Aldridge clattering into Neville Southall as he attempted to bustle into the penalty area. However, despite Everton's territorial domination, they had been unable to really threaten the Liverpool goal at all, and the game had really lacked quality. Trevor Brooking described the game as a 'stalemate', crediting the midfield players from both teams staying behind the ball as the main cause, but as the whistle went for half-time, it had been a desperately poor game of football.

Finally, in the opening minutes of the second half, Liverpool crafted an opening. The chance came through Peter Beardsley, as he cleverly dummied a pass into him by Gary Ablett, which caused the ball to run directly into the path of John Aldridge. Bearing down on the Everton box, Aldridge was clattered into by Pat Van Den Hauwe for a free kick just outside the box. As he turned round, it was clear from the look on his face that Van Den Hauwe knew exactly what he'd done. In the modern day, the foul could well garner a red card. In 1987/88, it was a free kick to Liverpool, and nothing more. Barnes took the resulting set piece, but his shot fell harmlessly into the waiting arms of Southall.

Still the game laboured, almost as if it was waiting to spring into action. As Steve Nicol hoofed the ball clear of the Liverpool area, John Motson gave the underestimation of the century by saying, 'Well I'm afraid there's not a great deal of style or shape about it just at present.' For a team that had been so gloriously attacking and fluid in their play, it was easily one of the worst performances Dalglish's men had given all season. Despite the poor performance, Liverpool did begin to venture forwards more, as Barnes and Beardsley began to find space and became more influential. It was the pair – whose signings had promised so much for the season – who finally gave the game the moment it was begging for. From a Liverpool throw in the Everton half, Gary Ablett delivered the ball to John Barnes. As Barnes side-stepped a challenge from Paul Bracewell, he played it inside to Beardsley, who simply played the ball into space with the inside of his right foot. With the Everton defensive line now exposed, Barnes ran on to Beardsley's through ball and fired a cross into the box, where Ray Houghton met it with his head to guide the ball into the bottom corner. As Houghton jumped into the air in celebration, all of the reds in Goodison Park, many of whom were behind the goal, erupted, as Houghton, Barnes, Spackman, Aldridge and Ablett celebrated. Chants of 'Liverpool, Liverpool, Liverpool' rang out from the away end as Liverpool managed the remainder of the game.

Bruce Grobbelaar's excellent goalkeeping halted the only nervy moment of the last minutes of the game, as he came out to claim a cross with most of the Everton players forward to chase the game. With the final whistle, Liverpool went through to the FA Cup sixth round, and still had the possibility of another double. The game itself had been so lacking in quality, and Dalglish summed it up perfectly, saying, 'Maybe the only bit of football in the match brought the goal.' Ian Rush was also asked about the game, and said, 'Liverpool didn't really play well today, but they still beat one of the best teams in the country.' David Lacey in *The Guardian* was hardly complimentary about the game, saying the goal had been 'out of context with the grey spectacle which had gone before'. Regardless of the performance, the bookmakers made Liverpool 6-4 favourites to lift the cup for the second time in three years.

Liverpool closed February 1988 in league action, as they travelled to Fratton Park to face Portsmouth on 27 February. The Reds were yet again unchanged, but Ronnie Whelan made his return to the squad, being named on the bench alongside Jan Mølby. Fratton Park was packed to the rafters, such was the continuing interest in Liverpool's still unbeaten side. Portsmouth were at the time unbeaten in ten games, and gave Liverpool plenty of trouble early on, but Dalglish's side quickly hit their stride, with Barnes almost scoring when he rounded Pompey keeper Alan Knight, but he was unable to finish from a tight angle. Barnes had received much attention for the do-it-yourself shaved haircut he had given himself prior to the Merseyside derby a week earlier, but he was clearly back on form and scored the opener early in the second half, although he certainly didn't intend his cross to deflect wildly in over Knight, following a challenge by Billy Gilbert. However, there was nothing flukey about Liverpool's second, as Peter Beardsley had the ball on the right flank and played it inside to Ray Houghton in the box. Selflessly, the Republic of Ireland international squared it to an unmarked Barnes, who stabbed it home. Ian Ridley in *The Guardian* gave real credit to Liverpool's defence – who had only conceded once in 12 games – including Gary Ablett, who had seamlessly slotted in at left-back alongside Alan Hansen.

As February 1988 ended, Liverpool remained comfortably top of the First Division, as well as unbeaten in the league. Kenny Dalglish's side now found themselves only two games away from equalling Don Revie's great Leeds United side of 1973/74, who went 29 games unbeaten from the start of the season. Liverpool's first two games of March 1988 would be against Queens Park Rangers and Derby County, and it seemed like nothing, not even QPR's 'plastic pitch', could stop them achieving the record. Even more tantalisingly, Liverpool's next league game after the away trip to Derby was against Everton at Goodison Park.

Chapter 12

March

THROUGHOUT THE 1987/88 season, Liverpool had been simply peerless. Kenny Dalglish's side began March 1988 so far clear at the top of the First Division that winning the league title had become only a matter of time. Breaking Leeds United's record of unbeaten games from the start of a league campaign remained Liverpool's only real challenge, with Arsenal, Everton and Nottingham Forest way adrift. Dalglish's men also found themselves through to the latter stages of the FA Cup, and on for an unprecedented second double in three years.

The Reds started the month on the road – after they took part in Sammy Lee's testimonial against Osasuna in Spain on 1 March – as they journeyed south to the plastic pitch at QPR's Loftus Road stadium. QPR had been the early pace-setters in

1987/88, although Liverpool had always maintained games in hand, until QPR's 4-0 drubbing at Anfield in October. It was a changed Liverpool side, with Aldridge unavailable, so John Barnes started the game up front, as Ray Houghton shifted into central midfield, and Craig Johnston returned to the starting line-up. Dalglish also handed a debut to 19-year-old Alex Watson, who partnered Hansen in defence, with Nicol shifted over to right-back. Interestingly, Dalglish even named himself as a substitute, though he wouldn't leave the bench.

On the day, QPR's astroturf pitch looked rather worse for wear, but Liverpool managed to come away with three points, after a Craig Johnston shot was palmed out by QPR keeper David Seaman directly into the path of John Barnes, who finished coolly. Dalglish was full of praise for the debutant Watson, saying, 'Magnificent. He surpassed all our expectations.' Nevertheless, it was clear that Liverpool were sorely missing the presence of Gary Gillespie, who had developed such a strong partnership with Alan Hansen. QPR had chances to score, particularly when Mark Falco was put through after some static Liverpool defending, but he put his shot well wide of Bruce Grobbelaar's goal. Still, the win meant that Liverpool had the chance to equal Leeds' record in their next league fixture at the Baseball Ground against Derby County.

Before that though, Liverpool returned to cup action, as they faced the young and promising Manchester City in the FA Cup sixth round at Maine Road. Gary Gillespie made his much-awaited return to the starting line-up, as Alex Watson dropped to the bench. The prolific John Aldridge was again unavailable, so Dalglish shifted the system to accommodate, as Craig Johnston partnered Peter Beardsley up front. The television coverage was held by ITV on *The Big Match Live*, with former Manchester City manager John Bond as a guest alongside Elton Welsby. He was absolutely glowing in admiration for the 1987/88 Liverpool side, saying:

> I wasn't always a great fan of theirs, but I am now ... I thought at times they were very negative, but they're not negative now, they've got a lot of very exciting players playing for them, and they're an exciting side to watch, and they play the game right. They work hard, tremendously hard as individuals, they work hard as a team, they've got a lot of flair, they combine that with good teamwork, and they're a magnificent side to look at, and I'm

delighted that I'm here watching them today.

Liverpool weathered the usual FA Cup away tie onslaught in the first few minutes, as the Maine Road crowd immediately roared into life following the kick-off. In fact, Liverpool should perhaps have been ahead early on, as Peter Beardsley spurned an early chance as he fired wide from near the penalty spot. Increasingly, Dalglish's side began to flex their muscles, particularly through the combination of Beardsley and Barnes, who often combined down the Liverpool left. As much as Maine Road continued to cheer for the team in blue, it was the team in red who constantly looked the more threatening. John Barnes showed signs of what was to come when he received the ball from Alan Hansen as he played the ball out from the back, and Barnes deftly turned the City defence with the inside of his left foot. As he bore down on the City penalty area, only an inch-perfect slide-tackle stopped him from being through on goal, but it was clear that it was only a matter of time before Liverpool took the lead.

Just minutes later, it happened. As Liverpool received a throw-in on the left flank, it was taken by Ablett towards Beardsley, who executed a one-touch pass to play the ball into the path of Barnes.

Fortuitously, the ball actually hit the England international, and as a result he controlled it and drove at the City defence, hitting the byline to cross for Houghton to fire home at the near post. On commentary for the game, ITV commentator Brian Moore simply said, 'It's Houghton, an amazing Liverpool goal, made by Barnes and finished off by the number nine. Astonishing goal.' So often pundits and commentators ran out of ways to describe the goals that Liverpool scored that season.

Manchester City enjoyed a good spell of pressure as the teams headed into the half-time break, but Liverpool's defence, with Gary Gillespie making a significant difference, had been more than up for the test, and the Reds went in 1-0 up. At half-time, the Glasgow Rangers manager Graeme Souness was interviewed, and he openly admitted that the Liverpool team he was watching that day was, in his opinion, as good a team as any Liverpool side that he had played in. Despite the absence of European football to allow the team to go down in European folklore, those in the know clearly understood quite how good Dalglish's team was.

Liverpool started the second half strongly, and Barnes almost made it two when he received the ball in the left channel, and as always dribbled past several defenders, only this time his shot went just wide of the post as he stabbed at it with the outside of his incredibly talented left foot. Barnes was in hot demand across Europe, and there was a Dutch television crew in attendance for the game, for no other reason than to show John Barnes playing. Indeed, Barnes continued to push, but it was Peter Beardsley who made it 2-0 to Liverpool in the 53rd minute, as he fired home from the penalty spot after Craig Johnston was brought down on the counter-attack after he rounded the City keeper Mike Stowell and looked sure to finish. In the absence of the regular penalty taker John Aldridge, Beardsley fired hard and low to the goalkeeper's right, and the ball nestled into the bottom corner. Liverpool should have had another penalty minutes later, when Beardsley took on a City defender after John Barnes ran about 50 yards and scythed through what felt like the entirety of the Manchester City backline, but the official didn't spot the hand used to tackle Beardsley as he headed towards goal.

City's Paul Simpson tested Bruce Grobbelaar with perhaps their finest move of the game, with his header forcing a top-class save from the Liverpool goalkeeper, but as the home side pressed forwards in increasing numbers, they were caught out on the break when Craig Johnston was put through to again round the goalkeeper, which made it 3-0 in the 77th minute. Johnston had at times endured a difficult season, having been dropped from the starting line-up upon the arrival of Ray Houghton, but this was a fantastic performance as he led the line in the absence of Aldridge, and showed his importance to the club as someone who could immediately step into the team and produce the kind of quality expected at Liverpool.

The Reds made it four through John Barnes, who once again picked the ball up in midfield and left several City players for dead. Barnes executed a one-two with Beardsley before firing home from close range. As the final whistle went, Liverpool progressed to the semi-finals after what Brian Moore referred to as 'another impeccable Liverpool performance', before suggesting it had become a 'habit' for Liverpool in 1987/88. David Lacey in *The Guardian* was, as so often, glowing about Liverpool's performance, saying they had played 'the sort of breathtaking football which has drawn the crowds this season'.

As someone who has watched each game Liverpool played, it's almost incredible to say that this Liverpool performance is relatively ordinary

The managerial 'Dream Team', Kenny Dalglish, Ronnie Moran and Roy Evans in the dugout together.

Kenny Dalglish wheels away after scoring the goal that clinched the First Division in 1985/86.

Liverpool's homecoming victory parade after completing a league and cup double in Dalglish's first season as player-manager.

John Barnes poses in the home team dugout for an official photograph shortly after signing for Liverpool from Watford.

Steve Nicol gets the Reds off to a winning start, clinching the winner against Arsenal at Highbury.

Mirandinha and John Barnes battle as Liverpool visited the North East in September.

John Barnes celebrates his first goal against QPR in a 4-0 victory.

Peter Beardsley scores the second as Liverpool beat Arsenal at Anfield in January 1988.

Ray Houghton opens the scoring in the 5-0 drubbing of Nottingham Forest.

John Aldridge and John Barnes celebrate Liverpool's second goal against Nottingham Forest in the FA Cup semi-final.

Kenny Dalglish roars from the sidelines against Nottingham Forest in April.

Bruce Grobbelaar and Ronnie Moran celebrate in the dressing room after the match against Tottenham Hotspur that clinched the league title.

Liverpool captain Alan Hansen takes in the applause of Anfield as he walks out to lift the league championship trophy.

Dave Beasant saves from John Aldridge at Wembley, the match that cost Liverpool the double.

when compared with some of their finest games in 1987/88, although it must be said that John Barnes tore the Manchester City defence apart on countless occasions, and the Second Division side had been simply unable to stop him. Regardless, the 4-0 win ensured that Liverpool were still on for the league and cup double, with only Luton, Wimbledon and Nottingham Forest as opponents that could stop them in the cup.

With progress secured in the FA Cup, Liverpool returned to their main objective three days later on 16 March, as they travelled to the Baseball Ground to face Derby County on a cold Wednesday night. Derby were struggling towards the bottom of the table, but they represented the last opportunity for any club of the First Division to stop Liverpool's march to equalling Leeds United's record. Dalglish's side entered the match 14 points clear at the top of the table, and with the league championship all but mathematically secured, the record had become the main focus on Merseyside. Perhaps most impressively, not only had Liverpool nearly equalled the record, but they had done so having scored more goals, conceded fewer, and had won more games than Don Revie's side did.

With John Aldridge again unavailable, Dalglish named the same selection as against Manchester

City, with Craig Johnston again chosen to partner Beardsley. The Baseball Ground pitch had certainly seen better days, with quite a bit of sand having been dropped on the playing surface, which caused the ball to bobble about as Liverpool immediately worked to get their passing game going. They played well in the first half, and should have gone 1-0 up, as both Ray Houghton and Steve McMahon missed good opportunities. McMahon's second was perhaps the best opportunity, as he blazed a volley over the bar after he was put through on goal by a lovely, lofted touch from Steve Nicol, a build-up that John Motson described as 'exemplary'. The home side's tackles were certainly tough against the league leaders, with McMahon and Barnes coming in for some rough treatment from the Derby midfield. However, as the half-time whistle blew, Liverpool were yet to break the deadlock, despite a Beardsley shot just before the break, as he cut inside from the left and fired low and hard, a shot that may well have had Derby keeper Peter Shilton beaten, but the shot also beat the post.

As the second half began, John Motson was once again full of praise and appreciation for Liverpool's play, saying, 'So much has been said and rightly so about Liverpool's flamboyant attacking play this season.' However, he also gave credit to the defence, adding, 'But what about their defence, 14 clean sheets in the last 15 matches ... terrific record.' Throughout this book, I have constantly tried to stress and highlight how attractive and free-flowing Liverpool's attacking football was that season, but Motson was absolutely correct to highlight how solid Liverpool's defence had been, solidity that provided the basis for Barnes, Beardsley et al. to express themselves higher up the pitch.

Early in the second half, McMahon was forced off due to an injury sustained in the first half, so he was replaced by Jan Mølby. Soon after, in the 54th minute, Liverpool finally got their breakthrough after Hansen, Ablett and Beardsley worked the ball towards John Barnes, who hit the byline, as he did so often that season, and crossed. A melee ensued near the goal line, as Derby threw bodies in the way of several Liverpool shots, but Craig Johnston finally finished it off by thundering home a shot that Shilton was unable to save. Liverpool then looked to take control of the tempo of the match, but Derby kept coming and, infuriatingly for Dalglish, they equalised with only five minutes remaining, as Gary Micklewhite crossed for Mike Forsyth to finish on the break.

Liverpool tried to push forwards to get a winner, but Derby expertly kept the ball trapped in the

Liverpool half, and in the end, although Liverpool equalled Leeds United's record, they did so with a frustrating draw. After the game, Alan Hansen said, 'We are all a bit sick – we just lost two points with a few minutes to go. I can tell you there are no celebrations in our dressing room. Everybody is just low about what happened to us.' The captain was clearly disappointed about the dropped points, and Dalglish echoed his sentiments, but was more positive about the record, saying, 'We were in control, and they should have been dead and buried. Normally we would have killed them off. Naturally it's a good feeling to have a record. When you are unbeaten in nine games it's good enough – in 29 it's just fantastic – but there are a lot of long faces in that dressing room.'

The high standards that had become a feature of Liverpool Football Club are evident in those quotes, the clear dissatisfaction among the team at the way the record had been equalled. Nevertheless, Dalglish's side *had* equalled the record, and had the chance to better it in their next fixture, against none other than Everton in the Merseyside derby. The footballing media hadn't been quite as glum in their reporting of the game, with Peter Fitton writing 'Kenny's Kop Kings roar to record!' and referring to

Dalglish's team as 'Invincibles'. *Match* magazine gave them another nickname, 'The Equalisers'. With the record on the line, Liverpool faced Everton four days later at Goodison Park.

John Aldridge was once again unavailable for the match, meaning Craig Johnston continued to be selected. However, he was played on the right, with Ray Houghton chosen to partner Peter Beardsley up front. Other than that, Dalglish selected what had become at that point in the season his strongest line-up, with Grobbelaar in goal, Nicol, Gillespie, Hansen and Ablett as the back four, McMahon, Spackman and Barnes as the other three of the midfield quartet, and Beardsley as the second striker. The groundmen at Goodison Park had done a fine job to have the pitch ready, after some torrential rain in the Merseyside area in the week prior to the game. Staff had been forced to keep the undersoil heating on throughout the night in order to clear the surface water that had collected on the turf.

On the day, Liverpool performed well, with David Lacey of *The Guardian* praising Dalglish's side for their performance. However, Liverpool's unbeaten run that stretched back to the beginning of the season came to a crashing halt at Goodison

Park, after a 14th-minute winner by Wayne Clarke, ironically the younger brother of Allan Clarke, who played in the 1973/74 Leeds team Liverpool were looking to surpass. The goal came when Reds keeper Bruce Grobbelaar came out to claim a Trevor Steven corner and failed to get his gloves on the ball, which caused a goalmouth scramble that saw the ball eventually roll into Clarke's path, and he finished with his left foot.

Tellingly, Liverpool failed to make their undoubted quality count in the game, as Lacey stated in his piece: 'Had Liverpool's finishing and final passes yesterday matched the quality of the rest of their football, we would have still been checking the annuals and manuals and working out the chances of Brian Clough's Nottingham Forest stopping the run.' This was certainly an accurate assessment of the game. Almost as soon as they had conceded, Liverpool pushed forwards in numbers and could well have scored multiple goals but for a poor touch or final pass that let them down. After the final whistle, Dalglish was clearly unhappy, and he later said, 'As the final whistle signalled a 1-0 defeat, I felt so frustrated I kicked a bucket placed outside the dugouts at Goodison. It was plastic, so the side buckled and the water shot up all over me. I was soaked, standing there dripping as I congratulated the other bench.'

In the same piece in *The Guardian*, David Lacey also praised the Everton defence, which he described as 'efficient'. Naturally, Bruce Grobbelaar came in for some significant criticism from the footballing media, as the *Daily Mirror* called him 'Grobbelaar the Wobbler'. However, Kenny Dalglish refused to lay the blame at the gloves of his goalkeeper, as he said, 'Any criticism handed out to any Liverpool player will never be done in public. Over the 90 minutes we deserved a little bit more than what we got, but there was no pressure on us because of the record, the only pressure came from Everton.' If Dalglish was disappointed to miss out on beating the record, he didn't let it show, and focused instead on what his team had done during the season, and continued, 'Our main disappointment is we didn't get three points. But our lads have been magnificent all season and any club would want to swap places with us.' The manager also highlighted that, while his team had failed to better Leeds' record with the defeat, the way his side had equalled the record certainly bettered the statistics of Leeds in 1973/74. Still, it was a disappointment on the red half of Merseyside not to have bettered the record, and undoubtedly more gutting to have failed to do so at the hands of their hated rivals Everton.

Nevertheless, when John Aldridge returned to the Liverpool line-up in the club's next game six days later against Wimbledon in front of over 36,000 at Anfield, Dalglish's side returned to winning ways, 2-1, with Aldridge on the scoresheet. The win – which was described as 'competent, rather than ecstatic' – sent Liverpool 14 points clear at the top with two games in hand over their nearest challengers Manchester United. Still, they had to fight to beat both Wimbledon and the Merseyside wind swirling around Anfield, and Wimbledon remained one of the teams Liverpool could still face at Wembley in the FA Cup Final.

Prior to the game, Gary Ablett had been given the Under-21 Player of the Month award, a just reward for his fantastic performances at left-back, having stepped into the back four with the sudden departure of Mark Lawrenson. The match had also seen an extremely rare sighting, as the player-manager gave himself a brief three-minute run out on a football pitch, and he received a standing ovation from the Anfield crowd. Although the unbeaten run may have ended as March 1988 finished, Liverpool remained extremely comfortable at the top of the First

Division, as they looked to push towards the double. April 1988 was to be a month that saw perhaps the greatest demonstration of what Dalglish's side were capable of, but we'll get to that soon.

Chapter 13

April

KENNY DALGLISH'S side began April 1988 well clear at the top of the First Division and on for an unprecedented second double in three years. They had swept aside all who had dared to challenge them throughout the 1987/88 season, doing so in a style that had captured the hearts of not only those in red on Merseyside, but also neutrals across the country. All that remained for Dalglish's side was to finish the league campaign – they required two wins to become league champions – and go for the FA Cup.

April 1988 saw them play Brian Clough's Nottingham Forest side three times, twice in the league and once in the FA Cup, as they faced Forest in the semi-final at Hillsborough. Before that, they faced Clough's side in the league at the City Ground. Ray Houghton returned to the team sheet, but it was Craig Johnston who got the start as the manager switched to a formation that featured five in midfield, in order to match Forest's 4-3-3 formation. In particular, Nigel Spackman was positioned directly in front of the back four, and constantly shadowed Nigel Clough. It was an unusually negative selection and performance from Liverpool, which only brightened once Peter Beardsley was introduced from the bench for Jan Mølby in the second half. By that point in the game, Liverpool were already 1-0 down following an own goal by captain Alan Hansen, and went 2-0 down two minutes after Beardsley's arrival when Neil Webb scored Forest's second. Although Liverpool pulled a goal back from the spot through Aldridge, they were more than deserving of the defeat after a poor performance.

Many questioned Dalglish's selection and tactical choices, but he said, 'No, no, no. Don't give us that crap about our fans. I don't believe that I don't have a responsibility to our fans, and I also don't believe that they would want to know from yourself.' Dalglish always had a reputation for being cold and prickly with the media, and he was certainly guarded in what he told them, and this comment from *The Guardian* is a perfect example. The manager may well have changed system and personnel simply to make things harder for Forest ahead of the FA Cup game a week later, but whatever the reasoning behind his choices, it hadn't worked and the defeat delayed Liverpool's coronation as league champions. The Reds wouldn't have much time to wait for their next game, as they returned to Anfield two days later to face Sir Alex Ferguson's Manchester United.

Dalglish returned to what had become his strongest line-up available. Grobbelaar retained his place in goal, and Nicol, Gillespie, Hansen and Ablett formed the back four. Houghton, McMahon, Spackman and Barnes made up the midfield, and Peter Beardsley returned to the line-up to partner John Aldridge up front. It was Liverpool's best line-up after the injuries to Ronnie Whelan and Mark Lawrenson, and over 43,000 were there to see the game, as tension began to build between Ferguson's Manchester United and Dalglish's Liverpool. John Motson, on commentary for BBC's *Match of the Day*, remarked as coverage began about how packed Anfield was, and that it had become a common sight throughout the league season. I've referred to it multiple times in this book, but Liverpool had really become box office in the way that no football team had in England for several years, and certainly post-Heysel. It was a glorious Bank Holiday Monday on 4 April, and certainly provided excellent playing conditions, with bright sunshine covering Anfield and Merseyside as a whole.

Liverpool started incredibly brightly, and kept United packed into their own half in the first two minutes but, when they lost control, United's Gordon Strachan launched a counter-attack from deep in their half, as he played the ball forwards towards the Liverpool back four. Uncharacteristically, Gary Gillespie only managed to nudge the ball forwards, and it fell to Brian McClair. As he combined with Peter Davenport, the ball was nudged past the challenging Alan Hansen, which left United through on goal. Davenport simply squared it to Bryan Robson, who finished excellently past Grobbelaar. After three minutes, Liverpool were 1-0 down to their hated rivals.

After a minute or two of looking shaky following the goal, Liverpool sparked back into life and pushed for the equaliser. Beardsley and Barnes began to show flashes of the kind of combination play that had simply torn defences to shreds throughout the season, and Steve Nicol began to get forward from full-back, a tactic that had so often benefitted Liverpool in 1987/88, whether he had played right-back or left-back. Ray Houghton also began to move into good positions, and started to threaten down the right flank. Houghton had been such an excellent and versatile weapon for Dalglish, able to go both on the inside and the outside as a proper old-fashioned wide player.

It was Houghton that helped to create Liverpool's equaliser. Nigel Spackman won possession in midfield, and laid the ball off to Gary Gillespie, who immediately played a one-touch pass down the channel into the feet of John Aldridge. Liverpool's number eight controlled the ball and turned in one movement, before playing it towards the run of Houghton. Houghton managed to shrug off the challenge of Bryan Robson, leaving him near the byline inside United's box. As he cut the ball back towards the penalty spot, Peter Beardsley expertly controlled the ball to move it away from the challenge of Steve Bruce, and fired it hard and low into the bottom corner with his left foot. 1-1. As Beardsley wheeled away in celebration, John Motson simply said, '1-1, and Liverpool fire back.' As the Kop erupted, suddenly all the momentum was with Liverpool, and eight minutes remained in what had been an enthralling first half. More was to come in what was labelled by David Lacey in *The Guardian* as 'The outstanding league match of the season so far.'

As chants of 'Liverpool, Liverpool, Liverpool' rang out around Anfield, they took the lead three minutes later. Steve Nicol, so often excellent, played a lofted pass into the box towards Beardsley. Liverpool's record signing turned and controlled the ball, evading a sliding tackle from Robson. As he reached the byline, he lofted the ball across goal, too deep for anyone to nod it in, but John Barnes himself volleyed the ball back across goal, reaching Gary Gillespie, who headed in to make it 2-1. Gillespie had been sorely missed at the back when he was unavailable in February, but he'd also done plenty of work in scoring goals, and this was his fourth of the season. Not bad for a centre-back. Once again, John Motson was in little doubt who deserved the credit for the goal, saying, 'Beardsley makes his influence tell again.' For a player who had received so much unfair criticism earlier in the season, Peter Beardsley had more than demonstrated his brilliance and just how worthy he was of wearing the number seven shirt made so famous by his own player-manager. The Kop was in full voice as the half-time whistle blew, and Liverpool went in 2-1 up.

Manchester United barely had time to breathe as the second half began, and Liverpool pushed on again. Nicol got forward on the right and stabbed the ball towards Houghton. As the Republic of Ireland international's cross was cleared, the ball fell to Steve McMahon about 30 yards out. Delightfully, he slipped the ball through the legs of a United challenge, then fired it into the top corner from about 25 yards. Again, John Motson's commentary is telling, as his response was, 'Oh I say! That's got to be one of the best goals of the season even by Liverpool's standards. What a belter.'

Sir Alex Ferguson responded quickly, bringing on both Norman Whiteside – who had put in a transfer request – and Jesper Olsen as United now had to chase the game from two goals down. Seconds later, United's Colin Gibson picked up a silly yellow card for kicking the ball away, as Ferguson's team were clearly rattled by the atmosphere and the performance of the champions elect. Mere minutes later, Gibson picked up his second yellow from referee John Key when he tripped Steve Nicol after having given the ball away to Liverpool's right-back. Seconds after Gibson left the pitch, Norman Whiteside picked up a yellow of his own for a poor tackle on McMahon, as United looked to have lost all their discipline and composure. Whiteside's tackle came in for some criticism on *Match of the Day*'s post-match coverage, as Jimmy Hill analysed how it had clearly been a premeditated foul, and condemned the tackle and others like it as threatening the livelihoods of other players.

However, United maintained a threat despite being a goal down, and they suddenly came back into the game after all of Liverpool's control and possession. Jesper Olsen hit the bar from an acute angle when Bruce Grobbelaar saved after a United counter-attack, and from the resulting corner the ball eventually came to Bryan Robson on the edge of the box. His deflected shot spooned to the other side of the helpless Grobbelaar to make it 3-2.

Liverpool had a chance to kill the game off when Aldridge's header was excellently saved by United goalkeeper Chris Turner, but in the 77th minute calamity struck as Peter Davenport received the ball with his back to goal and turned to play it towards Gordon Strachan, whose run had split the Liverpool defenders. One on one with Grobbelaar, the United midfielder tucked it into the bottom corner to complete an unlikely comeback. As Anfield was nearly silenced, Liverpool pushed for a winner but were unable to create the moments of quality that they had been able to earlier in the game through Beardsley. Infuriatingly, the game finished 3-3, meaning Liverpool faced a slightly longer road to be crowned champions.

After the game, Sir Alex Ferguson was extremely critical about what he argued was intimidation from the Anfield crowd, and targeted the officials, saying, 'I now understand why clubs come away from here biting their tongue and choking on their own vomit knowing they have been done by the referee. You need a miracle to win here.' There were also words back and forth between Dalglish and Ferguson, with Dalglish saying, 'My kid talks more sense than Fergie,' and Ferguson saying, 'It's been great, apart from Dalglish.' Although the two clearly have a deep respect for one another in the modern day, this was an example of the kind of animosity that Ferguson was capable of creating during his managerial career, and his pattern of creating an 'us versus them' mentality that created the ethos of the Manchester United teams that dominated the 1990s and 2000s. Still, Liverpool's player-manager gave just as good as he got.

Ultimately, the game was a missed opportunity. Victory against United would have left Liverpool's next league game – at Anfield against Nottingham Forest – as a potential title-clinching match. Still, there was much anticipation around Merseyside ahead of that league game against Forest, but first Dalglish's men had to play them at Hillsborough in the FA Cup semi-final. It should be said that with two defeats and a draw in their last four games, this was easily Liverpool's worst run of form in the entirety of 1987/88.

Dalglish named an unchanged team to face Forest, meaning that, unlike in the league, Liverpool now had their strongest line-up on the pitch to face Brian Clough's side. Forest right-back Steve Chettle had done a piece for the media ahead of the game, titled 'Barnes on toast', and suggested that Barnes wouldn't get a kick. Clough's Forest were a side that looked incredibly promising, with an average age of 23, making them one of the youngest teams to make the latter stages of the FA Cup. Indeed, their goalkeeper Steve Sutton was the oldest player in their line-up at 27. John Motson, on commentary for the BBC that day, billed the game as 'the team of today versus the team of tomorrow'. Over 51,000 fans attended Hillsborough that day for a match that demonstrated a clash of approaches, with Kenny Dalglish's more reserved demeanour against the not quite so reserved approach of the legendary Brian Clough. Liverpool wore their red home kit, with Forest in their away kit of white shirts, black shorts and white socks.

Forest quickly demonstrated their attacking threat with their 4-3-3 formation, as midfielder

Gary Crosby was put through early on, which forced left-back Gary Ablett to foul him and pick up a yellow card. Neither team really took control of the game early on, as the ball pinballed from side to side, and plenty of tough tackles went in from both sides. John Barnes had Liverpool's first effort mere seconds later, as he combined with Ray Houghton on the edge of the Forest box, but dragged his shot wide of the post.

In the 13th minute, Liverpool demonstrated just how dangerous they were. From a Forest goal kick, Gary Gillespie climbed highest and headed the ball towards Peter Beardsley, who had dropped deep off the frontline, as he so often did. Controlling the ball, Beardsley then immediately played the ball backwards to Steve McMahon, who marched through the Forest midfield with the ball at his feet. As Forest came towards him, McMahon played a wonderfully weighted through ball just inside the Forest right-back Steve Chettle. McMahon's through ball met the run of John Barnes and, as the Liverpool winger bore down on the Forest penalty box, Chettle made a last-gasp sliding tackle that brought Barnes down. Penalty to Liverpool. John Aldridge stepped up and put the ball in his usual spot, to the goalkeeper's left. Out of almost nothing, Liverpool led 1-0 in the FA

Cup semi-final through Aldridge's 24th goal of the season. They should have made it two just minutes later, when Barnes picked the it in the left channel and played the ball inside to Nigel Spackman, who had made a run from midfield, but as he moved into the penalty area his final touch was too strong, allowing Forest keeper Steve Sutton to come out and challenge. John Motson gave Spackman the benefit of the doubt, highlighting that the midfielder didn't often find himself that far up the pitch in Liverpool's system.

The match continued to be relatively open for a major cup game. At one point, Stuart Pearce found himself marching down the left and into the Liverpool box, before Liverpool countered and Alan Hansen played a cross – that went directly out of play – from the right wing. Liverpool continued to press and push forwards, especially on the counter, and keeper Steve Sutton was doing well to keep Forest in the game, as he made a fine save from a Peter Beardsley shot from the edge of the box that looked as if it was going in the top corner. At half-time, although Forest had played well, Liverpool had been the better team, and would have been happy to go in 1-0 up. Dalglish's side had demonstrated on plenty of occasions that they could take the game away from

Forest in one move, and they just needed one moment of brilliance in the second half to do just that.

Still, Forest maintained plenty of threat, and had their best chance of the game at the start of the second half. From a long throw-in, the ball was flicked on towards Nigel Clough at the near post, and his header – which Grobbelaar was absolutely nowhere near – went just over the bar. Heading into the game, much had been made of the youth of Forest's side, with Ian St John saying, 'In his short time as manager, Kenny has already shown exceptional qualities. He is sure to make it very tough for Cloughie's kids.' Despite that, Forest clearly weren't overawed by the occasion. They threatened again when Steve Nicol gave away a silly free kick just outside the Liverpool box, and Colin Foster climbed to head at goal. Fortunately, the ball was aimed directly at Bruce Grobbelaar.

Suddenly, in the 52nd minute, the moment of brilliance arrived. Gary Ablett picked the ball up and played it forwards to Peter Beardsley, who in one touch laid it back to John Barnes and floated out towards the left touchline. As Barnes played the ball back towards Beardsley and made a run, the Liverpool record signing lofted the ball – falling backwards as he played it – over the Forest defenders into the path of Barnes's run. Bearing down on the byline, Barnes crossed into the box, meeting the run of John Aldridge, who hit the ball on the volley to make it 2-0. In the moment of ecstasy after scoring, Aldridge belted the ball into the advertising hoardings, before the Liverpool players jumped on each other in celebration. John Motson, as he did, and continued to do that season, summed it up perfectly, saying, 'Exactly the same again, Liverpool come out of defence and snatch a vital goal … one of the best goals you'll see this season.' Dalglish's men had demonstrated their threat on the counter-attack throughout the first half, and following the restart the moment of brilliance they needed gave them the two-goal cushion they had been looking for. Chants of 'Liverpool, Liverpool, Liverpool' went up around Hillsborough from the travelling fans.

Forest again had Steve Sutton to thank as he kept them alive, again saving well, this time after an Alan Hansen pass had found Barnes in acres of space, and he played Beardsley through on goal. Barnes had been the player of the game, and the Forest defence couldn't get anywhere near him on the day. John Motson gave Barnes an incredible compliment, saying, 'Barnes's form this afternoon, a testament to the extra dimension he's brought to the Liverpool team this season.' So often when commentators talked about Liverpool in 1987/88 the admiration was clear, but none more so than the legendary John Motson.

Out of nothing, Forest made it a game in the 68th minute after a long throw was poorly dealt with by the normally secure Alan Hansen, which allowed Nigel Clough to stab in from point-blank range. Needless to say, Liverpool goalkeeper Bruce Grobbelaar looked none too pleased at the way the Liverpool defence had dealt with that set piece. Still, in the remaining period of the game, Forest, despite the fact that they pushed forwards in numbers and had plenty of the ball, were unable to create anything that threatened Grobbelaar's goal, and Liverpool played the game out quite well, managing the clock and the pace of the game. Despite the best efforts of Brian Clough's young team, they were unable to stop Liverpool progressing to Wembley and the FA Cup Final, and the possibility of another double. As Ronnie Moran and Roy Evans were seen shaking hands with Brian Clough as he headed to the dressing room, the Liverpool players celebrated on the Hillsborough turf, being joined by the fans, who streamed on from the stands. As Kenny Dalglish embraced Bruce Grobbelaar and Nigel Spackman in celebration, several Liverpool fans hoisted John Aldridge on to their shoulders.

Naturally, the media were glowing in appreciation of Liverpool, and the match in general, with the game being called one of the better FA Cup semi-finals since the war. The *Liverpool Echo* ran with a headline of 'Reds' Magic', praising John Aldridge's double for getting Liverpool through to Wembley. They also praised Barnes for his 'Star role in Reds' win'. Speaking to the BBC after the match, the Liverpool number ten stated that the movement of the players around him was what made this Liverpool side such a fun team to play in, and credited the team with playing football simply. Martin Leach for the *News of the World* also credited Barnes, saying, 'The wing wizard has had a memorable season, but he has never made a greater contribution to Liverpool's overpowering campaign than he did in this pulsating FA Cup semi-final.' It had been an incredibly mature performance from the whole side, but Barnes had stood out above all others on the pitch for his sheer class and skill. Their opponents at Wembley in the final would be Wimbledon, as they had defeated Luton Town in the other semi-final.

Liverpool's opponents in their own semi-final, Nottingham Forest, didn't have to wait long for revenge. Four days later, on 13 April, they travelled across to Anfield for Liverpool's next First Division fixture, as Dalglish's men looked to secure the league championship. It was a game that featured a performance that went down in history as one of the all-time greats. It was first against fourth, as Liverpool sat 11 points clear at the top of the table, with three games in hand on Manchester United after 33 matches. With the title in sight, the Reds did something quite special on that Wednesday night in April 1988.

Chapter 14

Liverpool vs Nottingham Forest, Wednesday, 13 April 1988

Grobbelaar, Nicol, Gillespie, Hansen (c), Ablett, Houghton, McMahon, Spackman, Barnes, Aldridge, Beardsley

Substitutes: Johnston, Mølby

Referee: Roger Milford

DALGLISH'S LIVERPOOL headed into the third match of the trilogy with Nottingham Forest in April knowing that the First Division championship was already effectively sewn up. However, in a season that had seen Liverpool rarely taste defeat, they had lost to Brian Clough's Forest earlier in the month, and were out for revenge. The win in the FA Cup had been a modicum of payback, but they hadn't beaten Forest as soundly as many on Merseyside had hoped. On a dark Wednesday night in April, Liverpool got the revenge they wanted, and English football saw one of the greatest performances in the history of the First Division. Liverpool's performance against Forest led to the game being called the 'Match of the Century'. Nearly 40,000 were at Anfield that evening to witness one of the all-time great Liverpool performances.

Dalglish again stuck with what was clearly his strongest available XI. Bruce Grobbelaar continued to dominate between the sticks, making fine saves throughout the season. The back four, which had been shuffled about consistently in 1987/88, was Nicol – who had excelled wherever he had played all season – Gillespie, Hansen and Ablett. Gary Ablett deserves some considerable credit for how well he had stepped into a back four that had been really solid until the sudden departure of Mark Lawrenson in January. Also deserving of credit was Nigel Spackman, who had stepped into the void left by Ronnie Whelan. Spackman may not have been as creative a player as Whelan, but he worked excellently with McMahon in a midfield that had plenty of graft and energy. Spackman partnered McMahon in central midfield, and Houghton and Barnes played on the wings. As always, Liverpool's front two pairing was the classic creator/goalscorer pairing of the creative genius that was Peter Beardsley, and the prolific goalscorer John Aldridge.

As Nottingham Forest kicked off playing towards the Kop, John Motson on commentary for the BBC said, 'So, the final part of the Liverpool/ Forest trilogy. Having seen the first two, I can only hope that this one lives up to what we've seen already.' Motson wasn't to know that this game would blow the other two out of the water, and his admiration for this Liverpool side, which had been evident all season, would only grow throughout the game, and his commentary reflected that.

Liverpool quickly picked up possession of the ball, and Barnes began to float into what would now be called the left half-space, as he did so often throughout the season. Barnes is so often thought of as just a traditional left-winger, but he really was so much more. He would often come deep to pick up the ball from the defence, and drive forwards in the inside-left channel. His progressive carries statistics in the modern game would be absolutely through the roof. Quickly, Liverpool began to play some lovely football, and stroked the ball around the back and into Barnes in midfield. Again, much of their possession play from the back would look ordinary in the modern game, but in 1987/88 so many teams played far more directly than Liverpool. It's the long-standing influence of the Boot Room on Liverpool Football Club, and it remains present to this very day.

As the game developed, while Liverpool maintained the majority of the possession of the ball, they remained one moment of quality away from creating a real goalscoring opportunity. Beardsley missed a chance to put Houghton through, and the latter himself made a poor pass inside that could have created an opening for McMahon. Forest continued to have the potential to be dangerous on the counter, and Nigel Clough demonstrated some excellent moments and wonderful touches that showed the potential he had in the late 1980s. The most concerning issue for Forest, rather than Liverpool having the majority of the ball, was the fitness of Des Walker. Having received pain-killing injections to enable him to play, he looked less than fit in the first ten minutes of the game. In direct contrast, Liverpool's own centre-back Gary Gillespie looked incredibly fit, and continuously marched into midfield with the ball to progress the play. His partner Alan Hansen played his usual game, picking the ball up and dictating from a position just ahead of the other defenders.

Liverpool displayed incredible energy throughout the first 15 minutes. At one point after a combination between Beardsley and Houghton failed to materialise, the pair pressed both the ball and the back-pass, forcing the Forest defender to put the ball out of play, with nothing on at all. Anfield erupted in applause for the sheer demonstration of effort from the two attacking players.

After the throw-in that resulted from the successful press, Beardsley picked up the ball from Houghton on the right-hand side, moved past two Forest defenders as he controlled the ball and turned at the same time, then dribbled past another into the box, but his left-footed shot went just wide. It was quite the warning shot from Beardsley, who created some moments of absolute magic in what remained of the 90 minutes. A minute later, a second warning shot was fired across the Forest bow, as John Barnes received a John Aldridge flick-on and forced a save from Steve Sutton at his near post. Barnes had been nominated for PFA Player of the Year prior to the game, and he clearly wanted to demonstrate just why he was deserving of that award. As Liverpool began to stretch their legs and noticeably took control of the game, Steve Nicol fired a shot that forced another save from Sutton after some nice approach play from McMahon. Unfortunately for the Reds, they found themselves unable to make that one moment count that would give them the lead in the opening exchanges.

However, in the 18th minute, that moment arrived. After a short spell of sloppy passing, Alan Hansen took it upon himself to bring the ball out from defence and stepped forwards into midfield. The captain laid the ball off to Ray Houghton, who floated in from the right flank. As he drove infield towards the Forest defence, he committed a defender to step out of the backline, which left a huge gap in the Forest back four. Immediately, Houghton executed a lightning quick one-two to march into the open space and finish past Sutton to make it 1-0. As Liverpool celebrated, John Motson made his first incredibly quote-worthy comment about Liverpool's style of play, saying, 'It looked simple, but done at speed, it's a great testament to the way Liverpool play.'

Quickly, Liverpool began to demonstrate that style of play. Barnes began to execute deft flicks and passes whenever he received the ball, and Liverpool's threat on the counter-attack became very real as Forest pushed forwards in search of an equaliser. He increasingly dovetailed with Beardsley, as Liverpool's number seven often floated out to the left flank, and Barnes shuffled inside. Increasingly, Forest found themselves trapped in their own half, as Liverpool executed their 'pass and move' philosophy. Their next shot came from Steve Nicol, as he fired just wide from the edge of the box after Forest cleared a Barnes cross.

Alan Hansen's performance was incredibly noticeable in the first half. Solid in defence as always, but his real strength was his progression with the ball, not just with his passing, but with his carrying as well. He may have been coming towards the end of his career, but Hansen remained an outstanding centre-back and had an excellent partnership with Gary Gillespie. As the man that Dalglish had chosen to take over as captain when his tenure as player-manager began, Hansen exemplified everything that Liverpool Football Club was supposed to be, in his commitment, professionalism and determination.

The fluidity with which Liverpool played that evening was simply outstanding. At one point in the 23rd minute, McMahon received the ball from Houghton and turned. The midfielder then passed to Barnes and swapped positions with him as Barnes moved infield and laid the ball off for Spackman. As Spackman moved forwards, he then attempted a lofted through ball towards McMahon, who had continued his run and found himself in the Forest box. Unfortunately, Spackman's pass was cut out by Steve Chettle, but that ten-second phase was a brief example of just how wonderful Liverpool's attacking movements were. Seconds later, Liverpool almost scored their second when Beardsley played Aldridge through, and although he was unable to escape the clutches of two Forest defenders and lost the ball, Liverpool's resulting press meant that they won the ball back. When Spackman squared it to Barnes on the edge of the box, his first-time outside-of-the-boot shot was saved by Sutton. Applause went up around Anfield for not just the press, but the instinct of Barnes to take the ball with the outside of his foot to evade a sliding tackle from the Forest defender. Motson commented about the 'range of skills' that Barnes had as he turned to get back into shape. Minutes later, he was also glowing about the work rate of the side, saying, 'The more you see Liverpool play, and the more you admire their attacking qualities, you continually find that those same gifted attackers are being asked to do a job back in defence, and it's possibly their overall work rate that has something to say about why Liverpool are the team that they are. There are no stars here.'

Still, Liverpool continued to push in the latter portion of the first half. At this point, Beardsley grew into the game more and more, dropping off the frontline to execute little passes and touches for runners from midfield – often McMahon. He almost created a second when he received the ball just inside the box and crossed to the back post. Aldridge was just unable to get a good touch on it, but did flick it on towards Barnes, whose point-blank volley was blocked by Chettle. Otherwise, it would undoubtedly have been the second goal. Once again applause rang out across Anfield, as Motson praised the fluidity and mobility of Liverpool's front four.

Seconds later came the best move of the match so far. From a Forest clearance, Alan Hansen headed the ball forwards towards Houghton, who flicked the ball behind him to Barnes with the inside of his right foot. Cutting in from the right flank, Barnes executed a wonderful change of pace, before slipping in Beardsley, who was completely unmarked in the box. His first-time shot was saved excellently by Sutton, as he tipped the ball over the bar. Minutes later, Liverpool almost bettered that move, as McMahon executed a one-two with Spackman in midfield, and marched towards the Forest backline, before firing a hard shot that Sutton was once again forced to save. The rebound then found Barnes, whose first-time shot unfortunately found the post. Again, there was wild applause around Anfield. McMahon had another pot-shot two minutes later, but blazed it over the bar.

Then after 37 minutes came – finally – the second goal. From a Forest throw on the Liverpool left flank, John Barnes managed to get a foot in to tackle, which caused the ball to run into space, towards Peter Beardsley. As he did so often in 1987/88, Beardsley allowed the ball to move past him to control it, taking two Forest defenders out of the game. Two touches later, he played a wonderful through ball to John Aldridge from inside his own half. As Sutton came out to challenge, Aldridge chipped the ball over him from the edge of the box to make it 2-0. Once again, John Motson's commentary says it all. As Beardsley picked up the ball, he said, 'Beardsley, oh, he seems to be able to find space and find Aldridge, and that is another super Liverpool goal! Peter Beardsley made it, John Aldridge scored it, and as with everything Liverpool do, it looked simple, but it was of a quite stupendous quality.' Beardsley's movement and pass really do have to be seen to be believed, and my words really cannot do justice to just how brilliant the goal is. Aldridge's finish – for his 26th goal of the season

– is absolutely fantastic, as he makes the difficult look effortless, but everything is about the pass from Beardsley.

Later in the game, Motson called it 'One of the best passes you will see, anywhere, anytime.' I've referred several times in this book to the doubts that several in the media had about Beardsley's performances earlier in the season, but at this point he was unplayable. The player-manager was certainly impressed, and later called it an 'unbelievable ball, sent through between the left centre-back and the left-back'. Even that was an understatement. As Forest kicked off again, cheers of 'there's only one Peter Beardsley' rang out across Anfield, and likely the red half of Merseyside as a whole.

Beardsley almost topped his moment of sheer brilliance just minutes later, as he picked up the ball just inside the Forest half and turned. As he moved forwards, he went past two Forest defenders, jinked his way into the box, dummied to shoot past a third and finally fired in a shot that rattled the bar. Despite his shot being just inches too high, applause rang out across the famous ground, entirely for the brilliant Beardsley.

Liverpool were beginning to turn it on. They almost scored a third from a free kick soon after, as Barnes laid the free kick off to Beardsley inside the box, and he flicked the ball sideways to Houghton, who forced an unbelievable save out of Sutton from point-blank range. McMahon would likely have scored from the rebound, but Forest left-back Stuart Pearce managed to push it out for a corner. As the Kop sang in full voice, John Motson admitted, 'Down the 25 years of success they've had here, I don't think there's been a better team surely, certainly not one with so much variety and invention.' Even Alan Hansen got involved, as he played a one-two with Beardsley that forced a last-ditch tackle from Chettle as the captain marched into the Forest box. Seconds later, Aldridge should have made it three following a lovely dummy by McMahon but a poor touch allowed Sutton to come out and challenge him. At this point in the game, it may only have been 2-0, but Liverpool continued to attack in waves, and Forest couldn't get out of their own third, never mind their own half. The pace slowed in the final few minutes but, as the half-time whistle went, Liverpool could easily have been 6-0 up based on the performance they had put in during the first 45 minutes. John Motson called it 'something close to a 45-minute football fantasy'.

Coming out for the second half, Forest had replaced the injured Des Walker with Darren Wassall, but other than that the mood continued much as it had at the end of the first half. Liverpool maintained control of the ball and the pace of the game. Forest played more brightly than they had at the end of the first half, but that really doesn't say much. Forest centre-forward Nigel Clough continued to get into good positions and was one of the few Forest players who acquitted themselves well, along with Stuart Pearce and Steve Sutton. Although the game was certainly more even, Liverpool still maintained their ability to seemingly score whenever they wanted to. Even Gary Ablett got involved, and ended up through on goal after being played in by Beardsley, only to be flagged offside. Liverpool's brightest moment since the interval came when Barnes intercepted the ball in the Liverpool half and dribbled at pace through several Forest players towards their penalty area. After picking up speed, Barnes laid the ball off to Aldridge, who squared it for McMahon, who was only able to fire directly at Sutton.

Then Liverpool came forward again in numbers. From a free kick, Steve Nicol dribbled infield from right-back past two Forest players and passed the ball to the overlapping Ray Houghton. He floated the ball to the back post, where it was challenged for by Aldridge. As the ball came back, Peter Beardsley took it under control and made one deft movement to commit two defenders, before firing at Sutton, who somehow saved the shot to keep his side only two goals down. From the save, Forest scrambled to put the ball behind. From the resulting corner, John Barnes passed to Ray Houghton. As he moved at pace down the byline, Houghton cut the ball back towards Gary Gillespie, who finished to make it 3-0 in the 58th minute. As Forest kicked off once again, the Kop sang loudly for Gillespie, who had played excellently in 1987/88, and had been sorely missed when he was out of the side.

Even at 3-0, Liverpool continued to push. Forest found themselves once again unable to maintain possession of the ball, seemingly lulled into a false sense of security by their spell of possession after the half-time break. As the momentum continued, Liverpool threatened to score a fourth. Incredibly, John Barnes nearly scored directly from a corner not once, but twice. Liverpool should certainly have had the fourth when Alan Hansen won the ball in midfield, played a one-two with Beardsley, before he looked to square the ball to Aldridge for what would certainly have been an open goal, but his square pass was inaccurate to say the very least, and the easy chance was missed. As the match headed into its final third, the only concern for Dalglish was a potential injury to Steve McMahon, who was forced to receive treatment – the magic sponge – from Roy Evans. Still, Liverpool continued to work, and their graft was evident, with at one point both Barnes and Aldridge ending up in the left-back position, with Aldridge making a snapping tackle on Forest winger Gary Crosby.

But when Liverpool came forward, they seemed unstoppable on the night. As they once again began to stroke it around the pitch, from red shirt to red shirt, Gary Gillespie found Ray Houghton, who had floated in from the right wing. Houghton played a square pass through midfield to Nigel Spackman, who began to dribble towards the left flank. As he did so, he played a ball forwards to Barnes, but the pass led Barnes out wide. As he controlled the ball at the corner flag, he nutmegged Steve Chettle, skipped past a sliding tackle, drove down the byline and cut the ball back to Peter Beardsley – who was one of several red shirts waiting – whose shot nestled into the bottom corner to make it 4-0 to Dalglish's side after 79 minutes. Once again, John Motson's commentary is telling: 'Oh, a glorious goal again for Liverpool.' With the fourth goal, Dalglish clearly saw an opportunity to rest players, and took McMahon off, replaced by Jan Mølby.

Still Liverpool pushed forwards. Nicol and Houghton played a lovely one-two that forced Forest into a pass-back, and Spackman and Barnes later combined to create a cut-back for Houghton that he somehow blazed well over the bar from point-blank range. Spackman had been incredible all game, and would have known that Ronnie Whelan, whose place he had taken due to injury, was rumoured to be on his way back. As Liverpool began their next attack through Alan Hansen, John Motson admitted on commentary that, while there were many opinions about Liverpool Football Club, he 'hadn't seen a better Liverpool side than this in the last 25 years'. Throughout the season, Motson's admiration for the side that Dalglish had built had been obvious, but in this, their finest hour, his deep-rooted respect for this near championship-winning team was impossible to ignore.

It had been a whole team performance, exemplified by the fact that when Forest striker Lee Glover was put through on goal in the final minutes, Steve Nicol sprinted and beat him to the ball to pass back to Grobbelaar. Nicol was without any shadow of a doubt one of the best full-backs in the country in

1987/88 and, like many other members of the team, this was one of his finest performances. Minutes later, he again denied a Forest attack, this time through Nigel Clough.

In the 85th minute, Dalglish replaced Houghton with Craig Johnston. Three minutes later, Liverpool made it five. Nigel Spackman yet again won the ball in midfield, and immediately laid it off to Peter Beardsley. Continuing his run, Spackman received the ball back from Beardsley as the Liverpool number seven played it through the Forest backline. All that remained was for Spackman to cut the ball back, and he did so to the waiting right foot of John Aldridge, who secured what was an incredible win for Liverpool, one that all but secured the league championship. As amazing as Liverpool had been in 1987/88, and as many goals as they had scored, this was the first time the Reds had scored five. As the Kop celebrated the final few minutes, belting out 'You'll Never Walk Alone', John Motson gave his final tribute, saying that the Liverpool anthem 'surely hadn't saluted a more complete side than this'. As the final whistle went, Anfield erupted in applause, fitting of the football they had just witnessed. One of the best teams in the country had just visited Anfield and been given a footballing lesson, one that demonstrated everything that Liverpool Football Club was about, and everything that Dalglish had built over the three years he had been player-manager. Fans littered the field to praise the side as they headed back to the dressing rooms.

Needless to say, the footballing media were in awe of Liverpool's performance. *The Times* reported: 'Liverpool set new standards in memorable show,' calling the win the 'most emphatic victory of the season' and saying the night at Anfield was 'unforgettable'. Cynthia Bateman in *The Guardian* reported: 'Liverpool turn on the title power.' Mike Ellis in *The Sun* called the performance a 'demolition job' and, finally, Phil McNulty in the *Liverpool Echo* called the game a 'football feast'. Even the BBC's World Service got in on the act, saying, 'Following half-time, you thought it couldn't be as good. It was. It was better. Another three goals from Gillespie, Beardsley and Aldridge again spiced with many memorable moves.'

These statements do justice to quite how incredible Liverpool's performance had been, but perhaps the most telling comes from Sir Tom Finney, who had been in attendance at Anfield. When he was interviewed for *Match of the Day* after the game, he said:

Well it's hard to describe actually because
I think that's one of the finest exhibitions
of football I've ever seen in my life, it was
absolutely tremendous and I mean, well
deserved, and you know, the skills and
the speed the game was played at was
absolutely tremendous and I came away
thinking I've been really entertained, and
I'm sure that all of the spectators here saw
an exhibition tonight that will never be
bettered.

It was the finest exhibition I've seen
the whole time I've played and watched
the game. You couldn't see it bettered
anywhere, not even in Brazil. The moves
they put together were fantastic.

Dalglish was also glowing in his praise for the team.
He called the performance 'tremendous' and said that
'every goal was a great goal'. He praised not just the
skill of his players, but also their work ethic, saying,
'Everybody can see how well we can play football, but
I think the fact that we work so hard is sometimes
overlooked in the high level of their football.' His
captain Alan Hansen said the performance was
'the best since I've been here'. An understatement
for sure, but one that demonstrates just how great

this side was. Later, when describing the game in his autobiography, Dalglish simply said, 'What a match!'

Without doubt, it was Liverpool's finest hour in a season of great performances. With the win, Liverpool required two further points to secure the First Division championship, and had six league games remaining. The title was simply a matter of time, but less important than that was the memory that Liverpool had left that night, one that would continue in the minds of all who attended Anfield on 13 April 1988. The 5-0 against Forest is a match that has gone down in history as one of the greatest, if not the greatest performance by an English side. Nottingham Forest were a good, young side under Brian Clough, and Liverpool made them look completely ordinary, such was the class and the verve with which they played their football. On that night in April 1988, nobody could have stopped Liverpool.

Chapter 15

The Rest of April '88

COMING OUT of the dominant 5-0 against Nottingham Forest, all that remained for Dalglish's men through the remainder of April was to secure their 17th league title. All that was required for Liverpool to do was win. They had three league games remaining in the month, away at Carrow Road against Norwich City, at home against Terry Venables's Tottenham and away at Stamford Bridge against Chelsea.

Against Norwich on 20 April, Dalglish stuck with his tried and tested line-up, save for the fact that Barnes wasn't selected due to a groin strain, and Craig Johnston instead came into the side in his place, a move that once again demonstrated the strength of the Liverpool squad that season. Perhaps most interestingly, defender Steve Staunton was selected on the substitutes' bench. Norwich were in the lower half of the mid-table area before the game kicked off, and Carrow Road was packed to the rafters with over 22,000 in attendance to watch what many assumed was the crowning of the new league champions. Norwich started brightly against the champions elect, however, as many did in the first minutes against Liverpool that season, only to fall away as their momentum slowed and Liverpool took control. Norwich did have chances through Trevor Putney, but they were unable to take them, especially thanks to the excellent goalkeeping of Bruce Grobbelaar, who hasn't received that much credit this story due to the focus on the attacking players, but he was fantastic throughout the season.

Liverpool did have chances of their own. Aldridge had a brief opening, but his snatched shot inside the Norwich box was saved excellently by Bryan Gunn, and Gillespie was unable to convert the rebound. Later in the first half, Peter Beardsley almost had a moment of genius, as he controlled a cleared cross to evade a Norwich challenge, only to hit a lovely left-footed volley straight at Gunn. Minutes later, he had a better chance through on goal, but blazed over the bar with his left foot. Liverpool's number seven had another opportunity later, just before the break, but this time only hit the side-netting from a similar position in front of goal. As the half-time whistle went, Liverpool would have been frustrated not to lead, but their performance had clearly been a step down from the heady heights of a week earlier.

A more unsavoury note is the fact that the Liverpool player-manager had to make a complaint to the police in attendance about the swearing he was repeatedly receiving from a member of the Carrow Road crowd. However, if anything, Norwich had the better of the game in the second half, with right-winger Ruel Fox causing some trouble for Liverpool down that flank against Gary Ablett. Liverpool did push forwards but without much luck or many chances created. In the end, when the final whistle blew, the score remained goalless.

Although Liverpool had played well, Norwich had definitely played well enough and done enough to earn a point against Dalglish's side. Alex Montgomery reported in *The Sun*, 'Kop marvels have to wait', praising Liverpool's performance in the first 45 minutes, and wondering quite how Liverpool had managed to go in level at the break. Stephen Bierley in *The Guardian* reported that 'Norwich delay the seventeenth crown', but stated that the league title was 'in the bag, it's as safe as houses'. Although mathematically Liverpool still required a point to guarantee themselves the title, it would have required a ridiculous turnaround at that point on goal difference for them to not be champions. Still, all they required was one point from five games.

Liverpool's next opportunity to crown themselves champions was on 23 April against Terry Venables's Tottenham Hotspur at Anfield. Almost 45,000 were in attendance at the legendary ground, as Liverpudlians packed in to watch the match that many assumed would see their team confirmed as the undisputed best side in England. Queues had formed from 10.30am ahead of the game, with interest in Liverpool Football Club at the highest level it had been since the 1960s.

John Barnes was once again unavailable for the match, meaning that Craig Johnston continued in the side. The decision of whether Barnes would start had been a tough one, with Barnes himself stating it had been 'touch and go', but with an eye on the upcoming FA Cup Final against Wimbledon, he was left out. Barnes admitted his disappointment to miss out on what was expected to be the clinching game of their title-winning season, but he understood the decision. The game also saw the return of Paul Walsh to Anfield after his transfer to Spurs earlier in the season. However, with only one goal scored in ten league appearances, he had found form difficult to come by in his early days at White Hart Lane. In fact, Tottenham had found results hard to come by as a team, and were in really poor form, with only one point in their last five games as they sat 14th in the First Division.

Liverpool started as brightly as the sunshine, and began to play their football, as Beardsley got involved in the flow of the game quickly, moving into channels on the right-hand side of the pitch, and it was from his work that a Craig Johnston cross found Ray Houghton, whose first-time shot forced an excellent save from the Spurs keeper Bobby Mimms, a former Everton player. Minutes later, Mimms was forced into another save as Steve McMahon, competing for a spot in Sir Bobby Robson's England squad, began to patrol and control the midfield. At the other end of the pitch, Bruce Grobbelaar had perhaps his finest moment of goalkeeping all season, as he swept up behind the high Liverpool defensive line, before playing a left-footed pass right down the touchline to Beardsley, who won a corner. Needless to say, the Anfield crowd erupted in applause for Grobbelaar.

Despite a first-half performance that was below their usual standard, in the 34th minute Liverpool got the goal they craved. Craig Johnston picked the ball up on the right wing and cut inside, laying it off to Ray Houghton. As Houghton moved towards the box, he played the ball out to Peter Beardsley on the right-hand side of the penalty area. Liverpool's number seven moved into the box before cutting on to his left foot, then shooting into the far corner to make it 1-0. Martin Tyler on commentary for Granada that afternoon stated, 'If that is the goal which clinches the championship, it's just the way that Beardsley and Liverpool have played their football this season … a masterly goal from Peter Beardsley.' Although Tottenham had shown some potential, especially through the involvement of Walsh, Liverpool went in at the break 1-0 up, with only 45 minutes to get through to confirm their league title, with Granada putting a graphic up that said 'Halfway to the title' after showing a replay of Beardsley's goal.

Tottenham began well in the second half, and forced some good saves out of Grobbelaar, particularly Chris Waddle, whose aggressive dribbling and fierce shot from 25 yards forced a good save from the Liverpool keeper. There were also some nervy moments, particularly when Alan Hansen challenged

Paul Allen as he ran into the Liverpool box, and may well have earned a penalty on another day. However, as Tottenham's momentum slowed, Anfield turned into a carnival atmosphere, with horns and singing ringing around the ground. As the 90th minute crept ever closer, whistles spread all around Anfield as Liverpool back-passed repeatedly – something that really is not missed in the modern game – in order to play the match out.

The 16,000 fans in the Kop began to sing louder and louder, and as the final whistle went, Kenny Dalglish immediately turned to embrace Ronnie Moran next to him in the Anfield dugout. Liverpool were now officially what most around England had known they were for months, First Division champions. The players took their victory lap around the pitch as the Kop celebrated, singing 'Liverpool, Liverpool, Liverpool'. Dalglish walked the Anfield turf, shaking hands and taking in the applause that his side so richly deserved. They had won the league championship, and had done so in a way that no Liverpool team had before. Their football had been so attacking and so fluid, that no other team in the country even deserved to be in the same conversation as Liverpool in 1987/88. The Kop's rendition of 'You'll Never Walk Alone' filled the ground as the squad took a celebratory photo together in front of the media.

Interviewed in the dressing room, Nigel Spackman said that the team would celebrate, but in a professional way, and Peter Beardsley admitted that the player-manager had already said that the team still had four league games left to play. However, the smiles from Dalglish demonstrated just how happy he was with what his team had accomplished that season. He stated that the win was just as sweet as his first as player-manager had been in 1985/86. Alan Hansen was then grabbed for interview as Bruce Grobbelaar began to cover everyone he could with shaving foam, and the captain said, 'It's fantastic scenes in the dressing room, but we've done it in style. We didn't play too well on the day, but we've scored a lot of goals and we haven't conceded that many ... we've played well all season and I think the league table shows that.'

It certainly did. With 84 points, 15 ahead of their nearest challengers Manchester United, and a plus 59 goal difference, Liverpool were more than worthy champions. The footballing media was as always glowing of Dalglish's side, with Fred Burcombe in the *News of the World* reporting 'Champions', and 'Beardsley Kops the golden title shot'. The *Sunday*

Mirror gave all the credit to Dalglish, with the headline of 'King Kenny'. *The Star* also wrote a piece revealing Liverpool's 'secret' after the title win, a secret that was revealed by captain Alan Hansen, which was simply to buy the players who caused them the most trouble. The article was imaginatively titled 'We Kop the Troublemakers'. Finally, the *Daily Post* ran with the headline 'Crowning Glory'.

Excitement was understandably high around the red half of Merseyside, and the prospect of the double was a very real possibility. As April 1988 ended, even a 1-1 draw with a struggling Chelsea at Stamford Bridge on 30 April couldn't dampen Liverpudlian spirits. Liverpool had just three league games to play, before heading to Wembley to go for their second league and cup double in three years, an incredible feat. Kenny Dalglish's Liverpool were undoubtedly the best team in the country, and April 1988 had proved it.

Chapter 16

Completion: May

AS THE final month of the league season began, Liverpool had nothing left to compete for, other than to finish the season strongly. A game earlier, they had won their 17th First Division title, doing so with relative ease from the chasing pack, led by Sir Alex Ferguson's Manchester United.

Liverpool's first match of May saw them collect the First Division trophy in front of nearly 38,000 against Southampton at Anfield. Alan Hansen raised the trophy in front of the adoring crowd, as well as the excellent trio of Dalglish, Moran and Evans, who had done so much to mould the 1987/88 side. Perhaps understandably, the match itself – which saw the return of John Barnes to the line-up – was a relatively lifeless affair of 'indifferent quality' according to *The Times*, as Liverpool demonstrated on relatively few occasions the kind of skill and quality that had caused them to be acknowledged as the undisputed best team in England, and one that was being spoken about across Europe. Still, they took the lead in the 41st minute when Barnes – as he had so often that season – received the ball on the left-hand side of the box and hit the byline, before cutting the ball back towards John Aldridge, who finished expertly. It was the kind of movement Barnes had made so often and made look so easy, in a season that had shown just how talented he was, as right-backs all across the country struggled to stop him. Liverpool were a post's width away from making it 2-0 in the second half as Peter Beardsley raced away from the Southampton defence on the break, but his shot hit the post and went wide as Southampton goalkeeper John Burridge came out to challenge. In the 68th minute, Rod Wallace volleyed home to frustrate and hold Liverpool to a 1-1 draw, but ultimately the Reds hadn't been at their best, and a draw was a fair result.

However, Liverpool were certainly deserving of the win in their second match of the month, as they travelled to Hillsborough on 7 May and demolished Sheffield Wednesday 5-1. Aldridge was absent for the match, so Craig Johnston deputised up front alongside Beardsley. Johnston and Beardsley ran the show, both scoring two goals, including three between them in the final ten minutes of the game. With a John Barnes effort added to their four, Liverpool were rampant. *The Times* gave Johnston plenty of credit for his performance alongside Beardsley, and questioned, 'How many managers would even toy with the idea of leaving out Johnston after his brilliant performance?' Significantly, the game had also seen the return of Ronnie Whelan, who was given 25 minutes in the centre of midfield. Nigel Spackman had been incredible in his absence, but Whelan added immense technical and creative qualities to the Liverpool midfield.

Journalist John Trevor in the *Liverpool Echo* called it the 'Liverpool super show', and said, 'The champions are in such sensational form that they look like turning the Cup Final into something approaching the eighth wonder of the world ... Liverpool are fantastic.' It's evident to see quite the level of expectation that Liverpool had going into the upcoming FA Cup Final against Wimbledon, as everyone around the country expected another champagne performance to demonstrate the brilliance with which they had dominated English football that season. It was a fair expectation.

Liverpool's 40th and final match of the league season saw them welcome Luton Town to Anfield.

Over 30,000 were in attendance on a Monday night. John Aldridge returned, but Peter Beardsley was missing as Liverpool looked to end the season in style. It certainly looked as if that would be true early on as they took the lead in the 17th minute when John Aldridge executed a wonderful overhead kick into the bottom corner from a Ray Houghton cross. Liverpool in no way looked to conserve energy for the upcoming final, demonstrated by the fact that McMahon received a booking early on for what Cynthia Bateman referred to as a 'crunching tackle' on David Oldfield. Nevertheless, Liverpool continued to demonstrate their style and skill, but in the 30th minute Rob Johnson beat Steve McMahon to the ball and played an excellent outside-of-the-foot pass through the Liverpool backline to Oldfield, who finished well past Bruce Grobbelaar in the Liverpool net.

Liverpool quickly regained their dominance, but were unable to find a winning goal. Instead, the Anfield crowd had to settle for half an hour of Kenny Dalglish, as he came on to replace Craig Johnston to thunderous applause from the Anfield faithful. Infuriatingly for the Reds, they ended the game down to ten men, as Nigel Spackman and Gary Gillespie clashed heads and had to be taken off after

75 minutes, with the Reds having only one remaining substitute to bring on in Kevin MacDonald.

Both injured players needed treatment and stitches ahead of the FA Cup Final. John Keith in the *Daily Express* reported 'Double Trouble' and highlighted the clash of heads between Gillespie and Spackman and suggested that their pair could be a doubt for the final. Cynthia Bateman in *The Guardian* reported, 'Blow to morale', which might have been an exaggeration. Clearly, Liverpool hadn't ended the season with the festival of football they might have hoped for, but they had still been unbeaten all month and had demonstrated that their ability to blow teams away remained just as strong with the 5-1 win over Sheffield Wednesday.

With a total of 90 points, Liverpool were the champions of the First Division. Dalglish's side had played 40, won 26, drawn 12 and lost two. They had scored 87 goals, by far the best record in the league, and conceded 24, with only Everton coming close defensively. It was a dominant league season, perhaps the most dominant in the history of English football. No other team had even come close to matching Liverpool in 1987/88, and all that remained was to secure the double by winning the FA Cup.

Chapter 17

Liverpool vs Wimbledon, FA Cup Final

Grobbelaar, Nicol, Gillespie, Hansen (c), Ablett, Houghton, McMahon, Spackman, Barnes, Aldridge, Beardsley

Substitutes: Johnston, Mølby

Referee: Brian Hill

LIVERPOOL'S 1987/88 season ended with the final game of the season, the FA Cup Final. Their opponents were Wimbledon, plucky underdogs, who had fought – in many cases literally – their way through to the biggest game in their club's history. Needless to say, given the stature of their opponents and the quality of Liverpool's football that season, the Reds went into the game as one of the biggest favourites in an FA Cup Final since before the Second World

War. In a pre-match preview, John Sadler wrote in *The Sun* that he 'predicted a Wembley slaughter', and the setting was right for the whole world to admire 'Dalglish's Diamonds'. In an interview in another section of the same newspaper, John Barnes stated he wanted to be 'the next Pelé' and aimed to be one of the best footballers in the world. Barnes was at that point clearly the undisputed player of the year in the eyes of football fans and the media, and the stage appeared to be set for him – and Liverpool – to prove their sheer brilliance once again. So many magazines and newspapers rated Liverpool's team as far outshining Wimbledon's in terms of quality and talent – a judgement that wasn't incorrect.

Fortunately for Liverpool, both Gary Gillespie – who wore bandaging on his head – and Nigel Spackman returned to the starting line-up, which was clearly Dalglish's strongest towards the end of the season. It was one of experience – only Ablett and Beardsley hadn't played in a major cup final before. To demonstrate quite how significant the rebuild at Liverpool had been, the line-up featured only three players from the 1985/86 double-winning side, Bruce Grobbelaar, Steve Nicol and Alan Hansen. In the tunnel prior to kick-off, there were accusations of verbal abuse from the Wimbledon players towards the Liverpool side. After the game, Dalglish looked to tone down those accusations, saying, 'Wimbledon had never been to Wembley in the top flight before. They were so nervous that shouting was the only way to get rid of their nerves. We knew it was going to happen. The intimidation in the tunnel was nothing. All Wimbledon did was shout.' Nevertheless, intimidation and physicality were a key element of that Wimbledon side, and Liverpool had to tackle it the entire afternoon.

There were some warning signs early on. Gary Ablett, who had so excellently stepped into the team following the departure of Mark Lawrenson, was caught in possession on the edge of his box, which led to a shot by John Fashanu. It was fortunately saved easily by Grobbelaar, but it suggested the kind of afternoon this great Liverpool side were about to have. On commentary for the BBC, John Motson stated, 'You'll notice that Wimbledon's forward players do hustle the opposing defenders when they're in possession.' Pressing from the front is so much part of the modern game now, but back in the 1980s it was a genuinely revolutionary tactic to press not only the midfield but the backline as well. Still, as the first half progressed, Liverpool maintained plenty of threat, mainly through Barnes and Beardsley.

The game continued to be physical, with plenty of hard challenges going in. Steve McMahon received treatment from Roy Evans after a scramble just outside the Liverpool box, and he was clattered mere minutes later by Vinnie Jones, who arrived for the tackle a good half a second after McMahon had played a pass to the left wing. Incredibly to the modern viewer, Jones received no booking for the challenge. He had been a key player for Wimbledon throughout the first period, not only in providing steel in midfield but also in the use of his long throw-in. Motson made comment of how quiet the start had been from Liverpool, which demonstrated how difficult Wimbledon were making it, along with the stifling heat in London that day.

Then Liverpool roared into life. Peter Beardsley picked up the ball on the right flank and floated inside, beating two Wimbledon defenders, which allowed Ray Houghton to overlap him. As he did, Beardsley played the ball through the Wimbledon defence, causing them to scramble back for the first time in the game. As Houghton cut the ball back across goal, Aldridge shot but it was saved by Dave Beasant. As Barnes followed up, his lightning-fast effort hit the post from point-blank range. Infuriatingly, Liverpool had failed to score.

With something to react to, the Reds inside Wembley began to chant 'Liverpool, Liverpool, Liverpool'. Minutes later, Liverpool had the ball in the back of the net through Beardsley, but the goal was chalked off due to a foul from Andy Thorn on the 'scorer'. Brian Hill, the official on the day, should have given the advantage to Beardsley as he went through on goal, but blew his whistle immediately when Beardsley was fouled. Of course, Beardsley, Dalglish and the rest of the Liverpool bench were absolutely furious at the decision, which should have put Liverpool 1-0 up.

Still, Wimbledon continued to play their game, going extremely long from goal kicks through Dave Beasant, whose kicks could reach the Liverpool box. John Motson gave credit to Wimbledon on commentary, stating that he believed too much had been made of the contrast in styles, and that Wimbledon had played some nice football at times, but the directness of their play was evident. As Motson said that, a long kick by Beasant was headed down to Lawrie Sanchez, who played the ball out to left-back Terry Phelan. As he ran to the byline, he was challenged by Steve Nicol, whose solid defending somehow received a flag from the linesman on that side, and a free kick for Wimbledon in basically the same position as a corner. From the resulting free kick from Dennis Wise, Lawrie Sanchez rose highest in the six-yard box to head into the corner of the goal, with Grobbelaar rooted to the spot. Incredibly, it was 1-0 to Wimbledon. The referee Brian Hill had cost Liverpool a goal from Beardsley, and a bizarre decision from the linesman had gifted Wimbledon the free kick that had given them the lead.

The officiating again came into question before the half was over when Aldridge was clattered by Eric Young in the Wimbledon box. As Wembley rose in accusation, no penalty was given. Liverpool pushed forwards through the remainder of the first half but, as the half-time whistle blew, for all their talent and skill they went into the dressing room 1-0 down. Still, as had been highlighted so often in 1987/88, Liverpool were usually better in the second half.

The Reds started the second period well. Wimbledon continued to play directly and frustrate them, but Barnes began to roam across the pitch and at one point ended up on the right wing, as he executed a glorious Cruyff turn that forced a corner. Unfortunately, the resulting set piece came to nothing. On commentary, John Motson continued to make comment of how difficult Wimbledon were making it for Liverpool, and how often they did this to opposing teams.

Minutes later, Liverpool had the moment they had waited for. Aldridge executed a quick one-two with Beardsley on the edge of the Wimbledon box and darted into the penalty area. As he stretched for the ball, he was clattered to the ground by Clive Goodyear, and referee Brian Hill blew for a penalty this time. As Wimbledon surrounded the official to complain about the decision, John Motson gave perhaps the ultimate commentator's curse, saying, 'Never has a penalty been missed in the FA Cup Final at Wembley.' Of course, Aldridge had been fantastic from the spot all season, and the vast majority of Reds on Merseyside would have put their house on him burying the ball from the spot to level the game. Aldridge took his run-up and went to Dave Beasant's left – albeit at a relatively comfortable height – but it was saved by the Wimbledon keeper. The score remained 1-0 to the underdogs after Beasant came out to claim the resulting corner. Only a few minutes later, Aldridge was replaced by Craig Johnston, a change that had seemingly been in the making for several minutes. meanwhile, Wimbledon brought on defender John Scales for Terry Gibson.

Still Liverpool attacked, though without the combinations they had demonstrated so effortlessly multiple times throughout the season. For every Liverpool attack, Wimbledon were more than equal in defence. In the 74th minute Dalglish made a more attacking change, removing Nigel Spackman's industry and running for the creative guile of Jan Mølby. Mølby had a season that was plagued by injury – he hadn't completed a full 90 minutes in 1987/88 – but he was undoubtedly a quality player for Liverpool over the years.

Countless times the ball entered the Wimbledon box, but as soon as any Liverpool player received the ball, blue Wimbledon shirts surrounded them and swarmed to stop it developing into anything dangerous. On numerous occasions this was true of Beardsley, who kept getting into good positions, but found himself isolated and trapped by the Wimbledon defending. The £1.9m man tried everything he could, but nothing worked. Each time, the ball bounced the Wimbledon way. Perhaps Liverpool's best chance came when Beardsley finally gained some space and played the ball out left for Ablett, whose cross found Barnes at the near post, but his header went wide from close range. It was a header that, in hindsight, Aldridge would likely have scored. In the final few minutes as whistles rang out around Wembley from the Wimbledon fans, Steve Nicol headed just over from a Mølby long throw.

As Mølby readied another throw, more whistles rang out. Unfortunately, the throw didn't have much distance and was quickly scuffed clear by Wimbledon's defence, as Brian Hill blew his whistle. Incredibly, after a season where they had swept aside all in English football, Liverpool Football Club had been denied the double by Wimbledon's scrappy, physical and direct performance. However, in reality Liverpool hadn't played well in the final, certainly in comparison to some of their greatest games during the season, such as Queens Park Rangers, Arsenal and Nottingham Forest at Anfield, and Newcastle at St James' Park. Yes, they had missed a penalty, but the BBC's commentary team of John Motson and Jimmy Hill had been critical of the decision anyway, and suggested that Aldridge's miss was divine intervention. Wimbledon played in their way, and played very well on the day, ultimately deserving to win.

As Liverpool collected their runners-up medals, chants of 'Liverpool, Liverpool, Liverpool' rang out across the glorious old stadium. Sadly for Reds on Merseyside, Liverpool had lost their final game of the season and missed out on a double that would have secured their status as the most dominant domestic champions ever.

David Lacey in *The Guardian* wrote 'Dons steal triumphant march', and said that Wimbledon's performance and the result would be long remembered by football fans, and called the victory 'historic'. Bob Harris wrote in *The Sun*, 'One Hill too many, Kenny', and said that Liverpool were outfought and out-thought at Wembley. He was certainly right with his outfought comment. Meanwhile, the referee Brian Hill received criticism for calling Liverpool 'a bunch of moaners', which brought his impartiality into question, and he was expected to be reprimanded by the FA for his outburst.

Heartbreakingly, John Aldridge spoke about the miss and said he 'felt like dying'. He had been fantastic throughout 1987/88, and certainly had nothing to be ashamed of. At the same time, rumours began to spread of the return of the prodigal son, Ian Rush, whose time at Juventus hadn't been as successful as both he and the Bianconeri had hoped. In another shock, Craig Johnston also announced his retirement from football, citing his dislike of the fame and the limelight, and his desire to move to New South Wales in Australia with his family. He had played excellently in 1987/88, whether starting or from the bench, and deserved the opportunity to end his career in his own way. His contributions for the club are well remembered by those in red on Merseyside.

So, with a disappointing end in the cup final, but plenty of intrigue already building for 1988/89 and the potential return of Rush, Liverpool's perhaps most dominant season ever ended. The FA Cup Final hadn't gone how Dalglish, or anyone at the club had hoped, but they had the chance for revenge in the Charity Shield that began the 1988/89 season. Liverpool Football Club never stood still, and the defeat made Dalglish's side even hungrier ahead of the most difficult year in the club's history. In terms of the football, that was it. Liverpool's 1987/88 season was over, and it was one of the best in English football history.

Chapter 18

The Legacy

IN 1987/88, Liverpool Football Club won the First Division. They played 40 league games, winning 26 of them, drawing 12 and losing only 2. In total, they amassed 90 points, scoring 87 goals and conceding 24. They fell at the final hurdle in their attempt to win a second league and cup double in three years, being defeated by Wimbledon at Wembley in the FA Cup Final. Despite their brilliance, Liverpool ended the season having only raised one trophy.

However, to reduce their performance in the 1987/88 season to purely trophies won and points achieved would be to drastically misunderstand their importance in the history of English football. At a time when English football was at its lowest ebb following the Heysel disaster, Liverpool provided a brighter face and a promise of a better future, without hooliganism and with style as well as the substance that had made English teams so successful in European competition. Names like John Barnes and Peter Beardsley had become respected across Europe, typified by stars such as Rudi Völler discussing them in the media, and labelling them as truly world-class players.

Moreover, the style of Liverpool in 1987/88 was the most incredible development. Their attacking play was so fluid and so relentless that they regularly blew teams away with attacking displays rarely seen in English football. Barnes in particular was glorious, and rightly won the Player of the Year award for 1987/88, but it wasn't a team of individuals, it was truly a great team, who came together at the right time. In his autobiography, Dalglish said:

> Although it was a different Liverpool side from previous years, they were guided by the same principles. The graft was as strong as ever. There was just more flair than before, with Barnes on the left. Barnesy had more skill than Ronnie Whelan, who moved inside. Ray Houghton was a bit more attack-minded than Sammy Lee or Jimmy Case. Some of the football was magnificent. Even I didn't know what they were going to do, and I was the man who prepared

them, picked them and sent them out onto the pitch. It was a very exciting team ... Liverpool won the League with four games remaining. We were that good.

Dalglish does himself an injustice there, however. He gave the players the freedom to express themselves within the Liverpool structure and framework, and that, along with the classic pass and move style Liverpool were so famous for, produced the flair witnessed in 1987/88.

The great football writer and historian Jonathan Wilson has made comment on the increased freedom given by Dalglish multiple times, especially on his podcast *It Was What it Was*, and has indicated that in a similar vein to that of the Romanian coach Ștefan Kovács at the great Ajax Amsterdam side of the early 1970s, that once Dalglish had given the team so much freedom, it couldn't be taken back. He has also suggested that this led to the eventual decline of Liverpool under Dalglish, although there were other factors such as players ageing – while Barnes, Aldridge, Houghton et al. had been great signings, they were all players entering their peak years, which would lead to a gradual decline. While Wilson's argument may be accurate, it cannot be denied that the 1987/88 side was the greatest flowering of style

Liverpool had seen in its history, and probably until the arrival of a certain Jürgen Klopp at Anfield. Liverpool played with passion and flair, and did so with a classically British style, but with elements of Continental panache. As a modern viewer, the games are a breath of fresh air. There's plenty of skill and technique on display, but the fight and the physicality also shown are often lost from the modern game. Watching the matches in 1987/88, Liverpool really did look like a complete team, who could beat you in any way they wanted to.

When the best teams in English football history are discussed, there are always the same teams that come up. When *Give Me Sport* ranked their top-ten title winners in English football history, Liverpool's 1987/88 side didn't even feature, despite the presence of two other Liverpool sides, the 1976/77 side and Klopp's 2019/20 vintage. When *FourFourTwo* did their own ranking of the 32 best teams in British football's history, once again Dalglish's side didn't even feature in the list. The 1987/88 Liverpool side is not only a disrespected side in the history of English football, but one that has been largely forgotten by the majority of football fans outside of Liverpool. This was a team so good and so entertaining that the BBC decided to dedicate the entirety of its Goal of the Season competition to Liverpool – Aldridge's second against Forest in the FA Cup semi-final won the competition.

Kenny Dalglish's 1987/88 side, and the players who played in it, deserve far more respect and credit than they have received. The played in a way so rarely seen in England at the time, and captured the hearts and minds of not only those in red on Merseyside but casual fans all across the country. Television viewership and Anfield attendance rightly shot up whenever Liverpool were playing, and they should be recognised for what they were, one of the best sides in the history of English football. It couldn't be bettered, not even in Brazil.

Bibliography

Select Bibliography

Dalglish, Kenny: *Dalglish: My Autobiography* (Hodder & Stoughton, 1996)

Dalglish, Kenny: *1989–90: Notes on a Season, The Record Breakers* (Reach Sport, 2021)

Evans, Tony: *I Don't Know What It Is But I Love It: Liverpool's Unforgettable 1983–84 Season* (Penguin, 2015)

Pead, Brian: *Liverpool, Champions of Champions* (Breedon Books Publishing Co Ltd, 1990)

Select Webography

https://anfieldindex.com/

https://bleacherreport.com/

https://www.fourfourtwo.com

https://www.givemesport.com

https://www.lfchistory.net/

https://www.liverpoolecho.co.uk/

https://www.skysports.com/

https://www.tandfonline.com/
https://www.thisisanfield.com/
https://www.youtube.com/
Official club website of Liverpool Football Club

Select Newspapers/Magazines

Daily Express
Daily Post
Daily Star
The Guardian
The Herald
The Independent
Liverpool Echo
News of the World
The Sun
Sunday Mirror
The Times